CONSUMER GUIDE TO

SHORT SALES

A PRACTICAL RESOURCE FOR
BUYERS AND SELLERS

DEAN ALLEN KACKLEY

ANKERWYCKE

Cover and interior design by Anthony Nuccio/Ankerwycke.

In 1215, the Magna Carta was sealed underneath the ancient Ankerwycke Yew tree, starting the process that led to rule by constitutional law—in effect, giving rights and the law to the people. Today, the ABA's Ankerwycke line of books continues to bring the law to the people. With legal fiction, true crime books, popular legal histories, public policy handbooks, and prescriptive guides to current legal and business issues, Ankerwycke is a contemporary and innovative line of books for everyone from a trusted and vested authority.

Printed in the United States of America.

18 17 16 15   5 4 3 2 1

Library of Congress Cataloging-in-Publication Data

Kackley, Dean Allen. author.
  The ABA consumer guide to short sales : a practical resource for buyers and sellers / Dean Allen Kackley, Esq.
    pages cm
  Includes bibliographical references and index.
  ISBN 978-1-62722-767-4 (alk. paper)
  1. Short sales (Real estate)—Law and legislation—United States. I. American Bar Association, sponsoring body. II. Title. III. Title: American Bar Association consumer guide to short sales. IV. Title: Consumer guide to short sales.
  KF697.S56K33 2015
  346.7304'363—dc23

                                                                                    2015003100

Discounts are available for books ordered in bulk. Special consideration is given to state bars, CLE programs, and other bar-related organizations. Inquire at Book Publishing, ABA Publishing, American Bar Association, 321 N. Clark Street, Chicago, Illinois 60654-7598.

www.ShopABA.org

For Susan

Important Notice: The information contained in this book is not intended to serve as legal advice. Nor does it substitute for real estate, financial, tax, bankruptcy, or other professional advice. This book and its author cannot and do not guarantee results.

The author's website is www.MortgageBriefing.com.

Contents

Preface

Mortgage problems? This book will help. It is the consumer's version of new federal rules for short sales for homeowners and landlords with underwater mortgages. It is the most current and important information available for owners in distress.

Professional advisors, especially real estate agents and brokers, can benefit from this book in two important ways. First, this quick guide will help them master the wide-reaching changes effective June 1, 2012. Second, it will benefit them by helping their prospects and clients to become better informed, encouraging assistance rather than resistance.

Relying on this valuable resource during a grueling but necessary process can shift the balance of power and help consumers gain control.

This guide will help people cut through technical jargon and specialized knowledge. Homeowners and landlords, and their trusted advisors, now have a simple, quick, and complete reference when working with lenders.

This book covers everything a homeowner needs to know and do to successfully complete a short sale under the federal Making Home Affordable (MHA) program and to work effectively with Bank of America, Chase, Wells Fargo, CitiMortgage, GMAC/Ally, and other participating servicers.

This accessible guide to short sales is invaluable for homeowners, landlords, and their professional advisors. Level the playing field and get the results you want.

Introduction

Short sales are not going away. Rarely known ten years ago, dismissed as too much trouble five years ago, they now dominate many residential real estate markets. They are a life raft for millions of underwater owners.

Short sales have made believers out of every real estate professional I know—who themselves were submerged not long ago by the delays, frustration, and sheer weight of unprepared lenders. Since then, both lenders and professionals have accepted the inevitable and have improved their systems and attitudes. Although the process is still slow (sometimes inexplicably, which is always frustrating), lenders and brokers are closing short sales—lots of them.

The federal Making Home Affordable (MHA) program started in April 2009 with a simple objective, some might say a naïve one: to modify problem loans so payments would be affordable and sustainable for distressed homeowners. A year later, seeing too many foreclosures and not enough modifications, the government initiated Home Affordable

Foreclosure Alternatives (HAFA), which organizes short sales and pays incentives to compliant lenders.

Begun to help homeowners, the federal modification and short sale programs expanded exponentially in June 2013 to include landlords and rental properties up to four units. Expiration was extended to the end of 2013, and later it was extended through 2015, but the problem will be around for at least another decade.

To solve the problem, values will have to go up, way up—as far up as they came down. In the meantime, millions of properties will change hands. Sellers will walk away without a dollar of equity or, if they pay attention, without a dime of liability. It's not a bad deal under the circumstances. Lenders—loan servicers and the elusive, impersonal, faceless mortgage investors who pull their strings—will take the hit; they will off-load as much as possible to the government or to pension funds or to foreign countries or to anybody else they can find; and they will either survive or go under.

The real estate marketplace is littered with the debris of greedy lenders, mortgage securities dealers, and loan originators, together with complacent or complicit borrowers and their fiduciary agents. Passing around blame for the problem won't help, although some accountability would. Still, here's a little advice that will help, from someone who has looked at the problem from all sides.

Relying on the generosity of banks to solve the problem hasn't worked. Just getting their attention has required new state consumer protection laws, federal Wall Street reform legislation, and the involvement of the Department of Justice supported by 49 states' attorneys general. We made a similar mistake when we relied on banks to lend responsibly in the first place. Homeowners in distress need to get educated. Then, instead of leaning on banks, they can stand up or push back, as their circumstances warrant.

Here's the situation according to the U.S. Treasury Department and my own observations:

- Value of equity lost by homeowners— $171 billion. This is not lost property value, only the portion lost by the homeowner, which amounts to everything that has been paid before the loan goes underwater.
- Underwater home mortgages—11 million. That's 11 million homeowners with no equity, hoping desperately for their homes to float on rising fair market values (FMVs). On the contrary, these are short sales or foreclosures waiting to happen.
- Foreclosure sales—about 60,000 per month. That's three-quarters of a million homes lost in a year.
- Sales by lenders of properties received in foreclosure—about 50,000 per month. This number was higher a year or two ago, but it has fallen below foreclosures, vastly more of which go to lenders than to private homeowners or investors. The result increases the institutional (shadow) inventory of unsold properties.
- Short sales—about 25,000 per month. At this rate, it would take 36 years to sell

the 11 million homes with underwater mortgages.

Before moving on to details about short sales and their consequences, let's look at the recently added or enhanced features of HAFA coverage that became effective June 1, 2012:

- All occupancy requirements have been removed.
  - Principal residences *and* rental properties are included.
  - Residential dwellings of one to four units are included.
  - Properties must not be condemned, but they may be vacant.
  - Seasonal homes periodically occupied or rented are excluded.
- Payment to the subordinate mortgage lien holder has increased from $6,000 to $8,500, at no cost to the borrower/seller.
- Up to $3,000 in relocation assistance may be paid to a borrower or tenant who must vacate.
- All senior and subordinate secured lenders are required to release borrowers/sellers from deficiency liability.
- Borrowers are allowed to make full contractual payments to stay current.
- The program has been extended to begin transactions by December 31, 2015, and close by September 30, 2016.

Homeowners and landlords: If your property is worth less than your mortgage, you need the information in this book, whether you decide to stay or go. Know your choices and their consequences. Do not wait for your lender to make the decision for you or for circumstances to dictate your actions.

Buyers: If you want the benefits of a short sale, you must endure the demands. You need the information in this book to prepare and protect yourself, to identify characteristics of the right property, and to know what resources are available to underwater sellers and, through them, to you.

Real estate professionals: If short sales are new or occasional transactions, you need the information in this book to direct clients toward HAFA or traditional options. This book can help seasoned professionals, too. Give copies of this book to your clients and prospects. You already know that working with well-informed sellers and buyers is far more effective than working with those who are uninformed.

For more information about the MHA programs, and specifically the Home Affordable Modification Program (HAMP), refer to another one of my books, *The ABA Consumer Guide to Mortgage Modifications: How to Lower Your Payments with the Home Affordable Modification Program.*

Wishing you peace of mind and a bright future.

Dean Kackley

Know the Players

Brief Introductions

Knowing the players is part of the game. Allow me to briefly introduce you to those who populate the short sale field.

Lender

You chose your lender when you took its money, or your lender chose you when it bought your loan or the right to service it. Following is an explanation of how certain terms are used in this book:

"**Lender,**" for the purposes of this guide, means one or more of the following entities, depending on context. It refers generically to the collective entity on the other side of your loan (your adversary). Most often, it means the servicer and those represented by the servicer.

"**Servicer**" means the mortgage company that receives your payments, bundles them together with thousands of others, retains its fee, and passes the remainder along to the investor according to the terms and conditions of the servicing contract. If you miss a payment, its collections department jumps into action. If you want or need mortgage relief (a short sale, for example), the servicer's loss-mitigation department joins the team.

The **loss-mitigation department** carries out the servicer's goal of controlling and reducing its loss on a defaulting loan. It solicits delinquent borrowers, or responds to their initiative, with offers to consider modification of the loan or sale of the property. This department administers the Making Home Affordable (MHA) program for participating servicers. Your application for a modification or short sale runs the loss-mitigation gauntlet.

"**Investor**" means the owner of your mortgage and of thousands, or perhaps tens of thousands, like it. A loan consists of the borrower's obligation to pay and, by extension, the recipient's right to receive payment. The recipient "invested" the loan principal with the expectation of receiving a return on its investment (interest).

Investors are passive, having contracted routine tasks to the servicer. Some might have the same name as the servicer, but they have very different functions. They manage huge amounts of other people's money, subject to securities regulations, according to representations and warranties of their investment prospectuses.

Except in rare circumstances, they were not organized to deal with individual mortgages and borrowers. They are more concerned with credit swaps, derivatives, insurance, and other hedges against loss and litigation. Further complicating decision making, some mortgages have more than one investor.

"**Insurer**" means either the private mortgage insurance (PMI) company that insured a loan with a high loan-to-value (LTV) ratio for an individual borrower, or a financial behemoth like AGI that insured a pool of thousands of loans against risk of default for an investor. Both add yet another layer to the decision-making process.

"**GSE**" means a government-sponsored enterprise, also known as the Federal National Mortgage Association or Fannie Mae and the Federal Home Loan Mortgage Corporation or Freddie Mac. After suffering substantial losses, they were placed into conservatorship under the Federal Housing Finance Agency in September 2008. At that time, together they owned or guaranteed about half of the $12-trillion residential mortgage market, easily the biggest investors. If one owns or guarantees your loan, expects its own variation on the MHA program.

"**Delegated authority**" means that the investor has given broad discretion to the servicer for making loss-mitigation decisions. Usually, this is good for implementing the MHA programs, and it typically applies to GSE-owned mortgages.

The **CFPB** is the federal Consumer Financial Protection Bureau established by Congress that opened for business on July 21, 2011. While its mission extends to all consumer financial products, general guidance and intervention with mortgage and servicer problems fall within its range.

Real Estate Broker

Whether buying or selling, do not attempt a short sale without the help of a qualified **real estate broker**. Home Affordable Foreclosure Alternatives (HAFA) requires the borrower/seller to list the property for sale with a licensed real estate professional in the community where it is located. Ask whether the individual agent has experience with short sales and with your lender. The supervising broker's experience also helps and might substitute for a less experienced but qualified and fully engaged agent. At a minimum, your real estate broker needs to understand the differences between a conventional listing and a short sale. The same goes for the selling (buyer's) agent.

Escrow or Closing Agent

Some call them **escrow companies** or **title companies** and others call them **attorneys** or **closing agents**, usually depending on geography. They take instructions from all involved in a sales transaction—seller, buyer, seller's (short sale) lender, buyer's (purchase) lender, and real estate brokers and agents. For short sales, they can be instrumental in helping to gather paperwork required by a short sale lender and in meeting its requirements.

Often, buyers select the escrow or closing agent after entering into the purchase agreement. For short sales, some escrow or closing agents allow sellers to begin the process earlier than in a traditional sale, enabling them to start short sale approval, especially for HAFA. Your real estate agent should be able to advise you.

Trustee

"**Trustee**" or "**attorney**" means the lender's representative. This representative conducts the foreclosure proceeding. In some states, a third-party trustee carries out the notification and foreclosure auction process under a deed of trust according to state statutes. In others, an attorney arranges a judicial foreclosure conducted by a judge. Once foreclosure starts, expect to hear from the trustee or attorney. The involvement of the trustee in short sales is marginal, except to postpone a foreclosure auction, and then it is critical. The trustee takes instructions from your lender. Make sure that your lender communicates effectively.

Others

Buyers and their agents need to understand how short sales differ from conventional transactions. A short sale buyer must be in for the duration. Be prepared for repeated delays. The best offer is the simplest offer. An aggressive price might work with few or no loan conditions. On the other hand, a ridiculous price probably serves only to waste time. Get prequalified for financing with a bona fide lender's preapproval commitment and proof of down payment. Submit proof with your offer, and add a brief statement of qualifications if you like.

Sellers need to be on board and ready, willing, and able to fully cooperate in meeting the lender's approval requirements. Avoid window-shoppers and buyers who want to make the sale contingent on a move-in deadline, the sale of their property, a very low down payment, or repairs to the property. For a seller considering an offer, the buyer's financing terms and qualifications are critical. Accept a lower price before enduring challenging loan terms. The same applies to property repairs: the fewer the better; having to make none is best. A general rule about multiple offers is to select the one most likely to close. In a short sale, you get nothing, so price doesn't matter to you. On this, you may agree with your lender: get it done the first time.

Landlords as sellers should be conscious of tenants' rights, usually imposed by state law. HAFA relocation assistance might be available for your tenant, if you run interference. Refer to the section titled "Relocation Assistance" in chapter 4, "Managing the Short Sale."

Landlords as buyers also need to be conscious of tenants' rights. An added wrinkle is federal legislation requiring 90 days' notice to vacate after foreclosure. Some states might match the tougher requirements for short sales, so check with an informed professional. Even in short sales, purchasers buy subject to existing leases.

Negotiators, who may or may not be professionals, intervene for a fee to negotiate with lenders about short payoffs, likely more relevant for subordinate than for senior loans. Although they are logical candidates for this role, some real estate agents might hesitate to assume it. The Secure and Fair Enforcement for Mortgage Licensing Act of 2008 requires certification of mortgage loan originators, which might extend to any negotiations affecting essential terms of a residential mortgage. Be wary of anyone charging a fee for an unnecessary service and of anyone who is not properly licensed or certified.

Facilitators are outside intermediaries hired and paid by servicers primarily to help with paperwork. Tried by some major lenders for a while, they seem to have little or no continuing use due to questionable results.

Summary

Like any real estate transaction, a short sale pulls together a variety of participants and functions. Unlike other real estate transactions, however, a short sale requires special skills, knowledge of related state and federal requirements, and lots of patience. Whatever role you play, make sure the other players qualify for the game.

CHAPTER

2

Short Sale

The Middle Course

Learning Points

- How does a short sale differ from a regular sale?
- What does a seller need to know before closing a short sale?

Short sales offer a middle ground between keeping a property through modification and losing it through foreclosure. They dominate large segments of the residential real estate marketplace, which has been littered in the past with debris from failed and frustrated transactions. Many underwater owners face years of negative equity, and some are staring impending foreclosure in the face.

A significant influence in the world of distressed mortgages is the federal Making Home Affordable (MHA) program. Its original purpose was loan modification through the Home Affordable Modification Program (HAMP). It then expanded to incorporate short sales through the Home Affordable Foreclosure Alternatives (HAFA) program. HAFA regulates short sales for participating servicers and lenders. It depends heavily on HAMP principles and, like HAMP, it endeavors to become the industry standard.

Chapter 3, "Buyer Beware," provides an important perspective for buyers before purchasing. Chapter 4, "Managing the Short Sale," details how to use HAFA to complete a successful short sale. But first, this chapter examines some of the broad issues faced both by buyers and, especially, by distressed borrowers when deciding whether to modify or sell.

What Is a Short Sale?

When a lender agrees to accept less than the full amount owed, it's called a short payoff. A short sale is a conventional sale that results in a short payoff when the net proceeds—price minus costs—are less than the loan balance.

The loan to be repaid consists of two parts. The promissory note creates the loan and the obligation for a borrower to repay it. The security instrument (lien, mortgage, or deed of trust) pledges the property as collateral and gives the lender a contingent interest in the property if the borrower defaults.

In a short sale, the lender agrees to accept less than the full amount owed, and it releases its lien so title passes unencumbered to the buyer. The question remains as to whether the lender will also release the borrower from the unpaid portion of the loan, the shortfall or deficiency. If so, the lender forgives the debt, and the borrower owes nothing more. Otherwise, the unpaid portion becomes a personal liability of the borrower, and the lender reserves a right to sue for recovery of the deficiency.

The borrower still owns the property during a short sale and, therefore, is the seller. As the seller, the borrower selects the real estate agent and lists the property for sale. As in any sale of a mortgaged property, the lender must approve the loan payoff. Historically, the selling price has been sufficient to fully pay the outstanding loan principal, and the lender's approval was routine. The difference between a conventional sale and a short sale is the short payoff and the lender's approval criteria and decision.

> **In a short sale, the lender may or may not release the borrower from the unpaid balance on the loan.**

CAUTION

Like a loan modification, a short sale is an alternative to foreclosure. Some mistakenly assume that the lender is the seller, but this can occur only after the lender acquires the property through foreclosure. This misperception arises understandably from the lender's significant involvement in approving the seller's circumstances and the property's value. Though not a party to the transaction, the lender plays a pivotal role in the success or failure of the sale.

Deficiency

When a loan is not paid in full, as in a short sale, a deficiency results. It's the difference between the amount owed by the borrower and the amount received by the lender.

The lender can forgive the deficiency, or the deficiency might be extinguished by statute. Otherwise, the sale of the property "strips" the loan of its collateral—the lien, mortgage, or deed of trust—and the deficiency becomes an unsecured personal liability. The lender then may sue the individual borrower for the deficient amount. If the lender prevails, the court awards a deficiency judgment.

The importance of ensuring that the lender waives its right to seek a deficiency judgment cannot be over emphasized. This is accomplished by statute in some states, including California. When a lender approves the short sale of a one-to-four-unit residential property, the law prohibits the lender from seeking a deficiency judgment. The prohibition applies to senior and subordinate lenders alike.

If it is not dictated by law, the lender's waiver is voluntary. To be effective, it must happen before closing the short sale. The waiver must be in writing, typically contained in the lender's approval letter and closing instructions, and often it needs to be negotiated. Without it, close at your own risk or cancel the sale. There are two alternatives to moving ahead with the sale: (1) foreclosure, which, in some states, extinguishes the liability, or (2) bankruptcy to discharge the deficiency liability. Before deciding whether or not to close, get qualified professional advice.

NOTE Talk to a professional about whether or not foreclosure in your state extinguishes the debt and, if there is a junior loan or lien, whether that could be settled or forgiven in separate negotiations. If all else fails, the debts might be discharged in bankruptcy.

The objective—debt forgiveness—can lead to tax liability, which is covered in Chapter 6, "Consequences." Exemptions might be available. Consult your professional tax advisor.

Considering a Short Sale

When I advise my clients regarding a short sale, several common themes emerge. Significant personal reasons compel some homeowners to stay with the property and modify the loan: family, friends, neighborhood, schools, sweat equity, pride of ownership, prospect of regaining lost equity, sentimental and emotional attachments, affordability of a modification, expense of moving and renting, deficiency liability and tax, credit record, a sense of responsibility, and similar considerations.

Others want out. The loan is unaffordable and the lender won't cooperate. The value has declined, equity is long gone, and the lender won't participate in a solution by reducing principal. Frustration has led to despair. These clients want a fresh start, even with damaged credit and spent resources. Knowing that a short sale harms credit much less than a foreclosure, they hope to reenter the market at fair market value.

Whether you stay or leave, try to set aside emotions and make an objective evaluation of your current circumstances and your short- and long-range goals. You have a choice among modification, short sale, strategic default, or doing nothing.

Modification brings your loan current and promises affordable housing, even if you expect to move in a few years and will still face a short sale then.

A short sale now might offer several advantages. Especially after declining a modification, HAFA and some lenders pay incentives for selling rather than proceeding to foreclosure. While the borrower is awaiting a short sale—or a loan modification—the foreclosure process might continue, but the actual foreclosure sale usually can be postponed, though not until shortly before the auction. Most already delinquent borrowers do not resume loan payments pending a short sale, and, after scheduling foreclosure, many lenders accept nothing less than the entire amount due.

Keep in mind that you are selling your property and must endure a lockbox, showings, appointments, finding a professional real estate agent, listing, selling, and qualifying for the short payoff. Also, reorient your attitude regarding price. A short sale means that you have no equity, so a higher or lower price doesn't affect you. Find a price that satisfies your lender, and try to get over your loss and what the market has done to the value of your property. A few prefer foreclosure despite the stress and credit impact.

> **TIP**
>
> Evaluate your situation and the pros and cons of the various options: loan modification, short sale, default, or even doing nothing for the time being. If you can't decide, start with a modification.

Most lenders do not consider a modification and a short sale simultaneously, though HAFA no longer prohibits it. Personal financial documentation for a modification usually covers what's required for a short sale, making a switch from a modification to a short sale easier than vice versa. If you can't decide, start with a modification and convert to a short sale. Find a real estate broker with short sale and HAFA experience, and ask your agent for guidance.

Timing is important because the debt forgiveness tax exemption for purchase loans secured by a borrower's principal residence expired at the end of 2013. Uncertainty about a further extension by Congress has slowed short sale activity. Talk with your qualified tax professional about the exemption, whether it will be extended, and how it might affect your decision to sell. Also, ask whether the insolvency exemption would substitute for the debt forgiveness tax exemption. And then, include your real estate agent in the strategy for closing accordingly.

HAFA

The federal HAFA program consists of guidelines and financial incentives for loan servicers (lenders) and borrowers to encourage a short sale or a deed-in-lieu to avoid foreclosure. Both alternatives reduce the need for potentially lengthy and expensive foreclosure proceedings while preserving the condition and value of the property. The program began on April 5, 2010.

Significant changes occurred effective June 1, 2012, consistent with the expansion and extension of HAMP and other MHA programs. HAFA now includes one-to-four-unit residential rental properties (which may be vacant), allows relocation assistance for tenants as well as homeowners, and increases the permissible payment to a subordinate mortgage holder from $6,000 to $8,500. Subject to lender discretion, HAFA no longer subjects borrowers to maximum income limits, although financial hardship still must be claimed.

Deed-in-Lieu of Foreclosure

Deed-in-lieu of foreclosure—euphemistically referred to as "handing over the keys"—for convenience is shortened to deed-in-lieu or simply DIL. Lenders accept a DIL and take title to the property subject to other liens and claims by subordinate lenders, the Internal Revenue Service, the local tax assessor, and other creditors. Most prefer foreclosure, which removes all such claims. Otherwise, both HAFA and lenders expect a borrower to clear the title of such encumbrances before the transfer.

DILs are discussed in the HAFA context in the next chapter. Though it is only a remote possibility, be aware that HAFA theoretically allows lenders to accept a DIL and then lease or sell the property back to the defaulting owner.

Summary

A short sale occurs when the owner sells a property for a price less than the loan owed on the property. Unlike a conventional equity sale where the lender routinely approves the sale by accepting the full loan balance, a short sale results in a "short payoff" and dramatically more lender involvement. While the lender assesses its loss, the borrower must make sure that no personal liability for the lender's loss survives the closing of the short sale.

One intent of the federal HAFA program was to set uniform standards for conducting and approving short sales, and HAFA eliminates the possibility of continuing personal liability. Borrower caution is needed, however, regarding tax consequences, which remain uncertain at this writing. Consult a qualified tax professional.

CHAPTER

3

Buyer Beware

How to Successfully Buy a Short Sale Property

Learning Points

- What are the advantages and disadvantages of short sales for buyers?
- What is the best way to build an effective buying strategy?
- What must your real estate agent be able to do?
- How does HAFA help or hinder a buyer?

A seller might have no choice about whether to sell short. A buyer, on the other hand, should carefully consider whether purchasing a short sale property aligns with financial objectives and personal needs. Although this book is directed primarily at sellers, with a slight shift in perspective most of the information in it can be adapted by buyers. This chapter will help.

The Long Short Sale

The single most common complaint about short sales is the length of time it takes to close. The second most common complaint is that too often short sales fail to close, especially after interminable effort, redundancy, and frustration. Do not even bother to make an offer on a short sale property if you have a specific and immovable deadline.

Since the mortgage meltdown began, real estate agents have staunchly refused to list or sell short sale properties, have grudgingly joined in what became the dominant market share of activity, and have begun again to eschew short sales as the share of conventional "equity" sales improves—all because too many lenders apparently still can't get it right the first time.

HAFA was supposed to change all that, and, to some extent, it has. However, experience varies. A Short Sale Notice (SSN) at the time of listing gives an acceptable price, which addresses the most frequent stumbling block. Guidelines call for prompt processing after a lender receives the purchase agreement. Yet, delays persist.

One mortgage investor might purchase the loan from another, or one servicer might transfer loan servicing to another. Though HAFA still applies, such transfers can interrupt processing or discontinue it altogether, requiring a restart with resubmission of paperwork.

The Need for Teamwork

A short sale differs from a conventional or equity sale because the purchase price minus costs is less than the seller's loan balance. In an equity sale, the lender simply specifies the amount needed to satisfy the loan, receives it at closing, and disappears into the transactional background. In a short sale, the lender takes a loss, decides what it thinks is reasonable, and plays a significant and influential role. Although the lender is not literally a party to the transaction, its involvement makes it seem like it is.

The buyer and the buyer's agent have no direct contact with the seller's lender. They rely entirely on the seller's agent and broker, although occasionally the lender will involve a facilitator with varying degrees of usefulness. My experience suggests that short sales succeed or fail essentially on a coordinated strategy orchestrated by a knowledgeable and motivated listing agent with the cooperation of an equally knowledgeable and motivated selling agent. Add a seller and a buyer who are both fully engaged, and the odds improve significantly.

The challenge, of course, is the teamwork needed among opposing parties.

Making an Offer

Short sale buyers can justifiably expect a better price than in an equivalent conventional equity sale. However, servicers and mortgage investors often defy logic while using apparently rational means to do it. Automated valuation modeling uses computer analytics and data gathered from comparable sales to arrive at a fair market value. It's best to know this number sooner rather than later, because it determines whether the minimum net proceeds after the cost of the sale will meet the lender's expectations.

TIP

If you are a buyer who is definitely interested in a short sale property, strongly communicate your interest as early as possible to the seller. The selling agent has no interest in holding out for a higher price.

If the seller and the sale meet HAFA eligibility, the listing agent should begin due diligence by soliciting an SSN on the seller's behalf. As discussed in Chapter 4, "Managing the Short Sale," in the SSN the lender agrees to important terms and conditions for approval of the ultimate short sale. Most importantly, it commits to minimum net proceeds from which an acceptable sale price may be determined, and it allows ample time to market the property and close the sale. Better predictability results and, though not a party to the SSN, a buyer benefits.

Don't expect the listing agent to reveal the rock-bottom price, but go ahead and ask anyway. The seller has nothing to gain or lose with a higher or lower price on an underwater property. The objective shared by all parties, and their agents, is a price acceptable to the lender. Thus, the most important aspect of an offer might be the sincerity behind it. If you are truly a ready, willing, and able buyer—as opposed to a window-shopper or bottom-feeder—and you are committed over the long haul, make sure the listing agent knows it. In doing so, you will have taken a long step toward building the teamwork needed for a successful short sale.

Buyer Financing

A recent trend witnessed owners of investment funds and all-cash buyers walking away with a lot of distressed properties. Deep pockets, dispassionate analysis, flexible deadlines, and contingency escape clauses have converted a significant number of owner-occupied homes into rental stock. Having driven up prices, the bottom-feeders are giving way to actual homeowners seeking properties and more conventional financial structuring.

Today, as was the case before the era of financing by smoke and mirrors, buyers must qualify to repay their purchase mortgage. They must satisfy three essential ingredients of good lending: first, ability to repay the loan from predictable income; second, willingness to repay the loan exhibited by a credit record of timely payments; and, third, commitment to repay the loan by pledging a cash down payment or equivalent equity.

Shop for price, terms, and reliability. You want an interest rate and fees that yield affordable, predictable payments; realistic criteria for which you really qualify; and a loan that provides funds when you need them, despite changes in closing dates, interest rates, and documentation.

Consider advice from your deposit or investment institution, active local lenders of any size, an established mortgage broker, and your professional real estate agent. Do not expect any special help from the seller's lender. It's not about salvaging a loan or converting a nonperforming asset; it's about cutting losses (loss mitigation) and moving on. Getting a purchase loan through another door at the same lender is purely coincidental.

If you need a purchase loan, the seller's lender will require evidence that you qualify. Be aware of the difference between a prequalification letter and pre-approval. The former can draw on a conversation, estimates, and anecdotes; the latter usually involves an application, supporting documentation, rudimentary analysis, and due diligence. Better—possibly essential—is an actual written approval by the actual lender, subject to identification and approval of the property to be purchased.

If you need financing to purchase a short sale property, don't expect the seller's bank to offer any kind of special deal—even though it's the one holding a nonperforming asset. It simply wants to cut its losses.

Depending on convention in your area, include with your purchase agreement the loan approval and a brief description of your motivation for buying, your interest in the subject property, and your time requirements, keeping in mind possible unforeseen, prolonged, and inexplicable delays.

A final word about buyer financing concerns the down payment. Like any smart seller, the short sale lender will want verification of the buyer's down payment, whether it's in the form of bank and investment account statements, a substantiated gift or award letter, or property listing and sale agreements. You will need to provide acceptable documentation to the seller for submission to the approving lender.

Property Condition

Rarely will the seller's lender throw good money after bad by repairing or improving the property before a short sale. The seller has no reason to incur any expense. The buyer should put nothing into the property until owning it. So, what happens when the roof leaks, the foundation sags, termites infest, paint peels, or appliances break or go missing?

Here's an excellent opportunity for the right buyer, meaning one with plenty of expertise, patience, and cash. Eventually, the short sale lender will approve a price low enough to compensate for poor condition and for the expense, effort, and risk the buyer faces. On the other hand, this is not an opportunity for the unwary.

Federal Housing Administration (FHA) guarantees have made low-down-payment loans possible, but they require the property to comply with building codes and to be in good physical condition. When a buyer needs an FHA guarantee, limit the search to eligible properties.

Cosmetic repairs, deferred maintenance, enhanced livability, new paint and carpet, updated appliances, and improved landscaping present economic possibilities and display pride of ownership. Contrast those with faulty electrical, plumbing, and HVAC systems; termite, dry rot, foundation, and roof damage; and previous "home improvements" made without building permits or code compliance. Leave the latter to experts.

Other Liens

Many short sales involve two mortgages: the senior loan, which is almost always the larger one, and a junior loan. Usually, the senior loan was used to purchase the property before its value declined. The junior loan might have helped in purchasing the property or it might have been added later to trade equity for a cash-out; in either case, the form could be a lump-sum equity loan or a revolving home equity line of credit. Before the short sale closes, payment less than the full loan balance must be approved for both loans.

A buyer should examine the title report of a potential property to ascertain whether the property has a junior loan and liens that will have to be resolved before the sale can move forward.

Other encumbrances that cloud the title might include unpaid property or income tax liens imposed by federal, state, or local jurisdictions; judgments filed after judicial action; mechanic's liens for construction materials, labor, and equipment; unpaid child and spousal support; delinquent homeowner association fees; and other assessments.

Junior mortgages, which are common, are included in the HAFA program for participating lenders, and they are covered elsewhere in this book. Other liens must be satisfied and removed before the sale closes and a clear property title can pass to the new owner. Lenders usually leave to the seller and the seller's representative the task of identifying and negotiating with such lien holders.

Lenders might allow diversion of proceeds from the sale to remove such liens. Some lien holders, including the Internal Revenue Service, waive the collateral interest in the property while preserving the underlying personal obligation of the seller. Most lenders frown on sellers paying lien holders directly with funds that might otherwise be used to pay the loan, though HAFA allows use of a seller's relocation assistance payment.

For the buyer, a wise course of action is, first, to complete a thorough and competent review of a title report before removing performance conditions and, second, to exercise caution before proceeding with the purchase of a property so encumbered. At best, expect unforeseen delays.

Tenants

Properties with tenants require special attention. The purchase of any leased property is subject to the lease. Whether it is for an equity sale or a short sale, the due diligence is the same, and the involvement of a professional real estate agent or attorney can be essential.

A tenant occupying the property on a month-to-month rental agreement, "at will," or without a written agreement presents a somewhat different situation. Federal law requires 90 days' notice before evicting a tenant after foreclosure, and many states have similar tenant protections. Such restrictions do not transfer automatically to other distressed transactions, such as short sales, but caution must be exercised to comply with state and local laws and judicial rulings.

In HAFA short sales, displaced occupants may qualify for relocation assistance payments of $3,000 cumulatively, shared by all units in the property. This incentive might help to clear the building, if necessary. Better is written confirmation by tenants of their understanding of lease terms including rent, expectations regarding continued occupancy, and an agreement to vacate. Such a statement, referred to as an estoppel, also would benefit from review by a professional.

HAFA Agreements

Buyers pursuing HAFA agreements should review the sections in Chapter 4, "Managing the Short Sale," under the headings "Short Sale Notice" and "Alternative: Start with the Sales Contract." The seller initiates both the SSN and the request for the sales contract and receives the short sale lender agreement about terms and conditions. The buyer, though not a party to these agreements, can benefit from them.

Short Sale Notice

The SSN, entered when the seller lists the property, specifies the lender's expectation about price and the minimum net proceeds it will receive after deducting the costs of sale. It also promises suspension of foreclosure for six months or more to allow effective marketing and to improve predictability for both seller and buyer, and for their agents.

Assuming the buyer and seller meet other conditions, the lender is obliged to approve the price agreed to in the SSN. A compliant offer can be made and accepted with more confidence and less likelihood of delays.

On the other hand, if the lender's expectation conflicts with market reality, the seller and the seller's agent can proactively appeal the price estimate with a strong comparative market analysis. Often, an appeal is most effective when combined with a strong purchase agreement that offers a price closer to fair market value. Ultimately, the lender decides, but odds improve proportionately with cooperation and transparency between the listing and selling agents.

Acknowledgment of Request for Short Sale

If short sale approval starts with a fully executed purchase agreement, the lender confirms receipt with the Acknowledgment of Request for Short Sale (ARSS), then begins actually approving the short payoff and accepting the magnitude of its loss. Without an SSN, the ARSS is often the first contact with the lender, initiating the value, price, and net proceeds analysis, and resulting in a longer process with less predictability. The lender compares the price with its valuation, suspends the foreclosure sale if scheduled, and reviews other conditions until satisfied. Allowed 30 days, the process can stretch longer, with the lender required to notify the seller of delays in 15-day increments.

Without HAFA, a lender's proprietary criteria prevail. Predictability varies, but buyers should anticipate more redundancy and longer delays.

NOTE

HAFA includes a procedure for disputing lender processing. While the seller must open the dispute, the buyer or buyer's representative can help with the process by working with the selling agent and providing a firm price offer.

Contract Contingencies

When entering into a short sale purchase agreement, a buyer must anticipate problems and include contingencies to address property inspection, time delays, the seller's failure to meet conditions, the short sale lender's approval difficulties, title issues, purchase financing complications, and other hazards. Many are addressed earlier in this chapter, but here is a quick summary.

Buyer Financing

Ensure that you have sufficient time to apply and qualify for purchase financing, if you have not already done so. Also, anticipate the need to extend your lender's commitment if the short sale encounters delays. If terms change or the commitment is canceled, make sure that you may terminate the purchase agreement without penalty.

Sale of Property

As a buyer, if you must sell a property, typically your home, for the short sale purchase down payment, then the further along you are in the process the better. This might put you at a disadvantage, but do not simply hope for the best. Include an appropriate cancellation contingency in your purchase offer in case your sale fails.

Closing Deadline

Even the short sale lender wants a target date, but implacable deadlines—even reasonable expectations—provoke frustration and too often arrive far ahead of the closing date. The result: a canceled contract, wasted time, hard feelings, and a possible foreclosure for the unwitting or unprepared seller. The message: don't get involved in a short sale if you can't be flexible; but if you still can't resist pursuing a short sale, include a contingency (and let the seller know as far in advance as possible before exercising it).

Lender Nonapproval or Approval of a Competing Offer

This is the seller's responsibility. As a buyer, however, hope for the best and plan for the worst, especially if the seller accepted another offer and yours is a backup offer. The seller will have an exit contingency, and so should you.

Cancellation by the Seller

Standard short sale listing agreements allow the seller to cancel if, for example, the seller wants to tender a deed-in-lieu of foreclosure to the lender or, outside HAFA, the lender proceeds with a foreclosure sale. In either event, the seller, too, must be able to formally cancel the sales contract.

Cancellation by the Buyer

Whether for an equity sale or a short sale, buyers include contingencies as safeguard against problems with the condition of the property, time delays, seller

NOTE

Experienced real estate professionals—brokers, agents, attorneys, and accountants—are essential in any real estate transaction, especially a short sale. Identify trusted allies early and involve them throughout. This book is no substitute for local expertise.

breach, nonapproval, title issues, purchase financing difficulties, and other complications. Here is yet another reason for industry-standard contracts and competent professional representation.

Summary

Buyers can benefit from the HAFA program if the seller and listing agent implement it. The lender's SSN, initiated by the seller, identifies an acceptable price and allows time to close, thus accommodating more conventional buyers. Consequently, most buyers would benefit from familiarity with HAFA features and from knowing whether the seller has implemented them.

Although most of this book speaks to sellers, the conversation is relevant to buyers, too. After reading this chapter, buyers and their agents can learn more by referring to the table of contents and to other chapters and sections of interest.

4

Managing the Short Sale

Home Affordable Foreclosure Alternatives

Learning Points

- How do short sales work under HAFA?
- How should the property's listing price be set?
- How can you get your lender's cooperation?
- What happens to the loan amount not paid?

The Home Affordable Foreclosure Alternatives (HAFA) program offers an important alternative to default outcomes. The program consists of two possibilities: a short sale that transfers ownership to a buyer, or a deed-in-lieu of foreclosure (DIL) that transfers ownership to the lender. For reasons discussed later, a DIL is rarely used, so this chapter emphasizes the HAFA short sale.

Initiating HAFA

Clearly, the bias of the Making Home Affordable (MHA) programs leans toward modification. Before lenders can solicit borrowers for HAFA, they must first be considered for modification under the Home

Affordable Modification Program (HAMP). If HAMP fails, then the lender must consider a borrower for HAFA eligibility. Borrowers may initiate HAFA anytime by informing their lender of their desire to do so. To summarize, lenders must consider a borrower's eligibility for HAFA within 30 days after the borrower:

- Fails to qualify for a trial modification;
- Fails to complete a trial modification;
- Misses two consecutive permanent HAMP modification payments; or
- Requests a short sale by verbal or written expression of interest.

MHA requires lenders to respond to a borrower's expression of interest within 30 days, and it urges lenders to use HAFA before using their own proprietary short sale programs.

Lenders and HAFA

Within HAFA guidelines, lenders exercise considerable discretion, primarily to accommodate external forces. Variances in state laws and servicing contracts with mortgage investors might result in different outcomes for similar loans. To ensure fairness and all possible consistency, HAFA expects servicers to develop a written HAFA policy that describes such variances and their resolution.

Here are some of the issues that a servicer's HAFA policy might cover. This list is a good quick summary of issues that a borrower or real estate agent might encounter.

- How to decide on an acceptable sales price
- How to reconcile differences between the lender's valuation and the listing price
- How to determine settlement amounts to satisfy junior loans
- Who negotiates with junior lien holders and other subordinate lien holders
- Whether and how to consider the borrower's income
- Whether a borrower (seller) may lease back or repurchase the property
- Under what conditions an occupant may continue to occupy the property
- How to validate occupancy of the owner or tenant for relocation assistance

A list of lenders and links to their policy statements can be found at: http://www.makinghome affordable.gov/for-partners/ understanding-guidelines/Pages/ HAFAMatrix.aspx.

Servicers must decide how to deal with such issues. Then, they must present that information, along with a description of their other procedures, in a published HAFA policy, summarized in a HAFA matrix posted on their website. Some use a standard MHA format that helps to present the information in a uniform way.

A Borrower's Eligibility for HAFA

If a borrower previously requested HAMP, and the lender received the signed Request for Mortgage Assistance (RMA), HAFA requires no other financial or hardship information. At their discretion, however, servicers may request additional and updated information.

If a borrower not previously considered for HAMP requests a short sale, then the borrower must submit an RMA or Hardship Affidavit, along with the listing and purchase agreements when available. Anyone seeking relocation assistance must submit a Dodd–Frank Certification.[i] Despite minimal HAFA requirements, expect most lenders to require other qualifying documentation, which their HAFA policy matrix might outline on their website.

The lender begins by determining the borrower's HAFA eligibility. All HAFA eligibility criteria are included in HAMP, though not all HAMP criteria are required for HAFA. Most notable is the absence of the monthly mortgage payment ratio.[ii] HAMP Tier 1 for homeowners requires a premodification ratio greater than 31 percent. HAFA eligibility ignores the borrower's income, leaving its consideration to servicer discretion. Again, check your lender's HAFA policy matrix.

Here are specific HAFA eligibility criteria:

1. The mortgage must be a first lien, senior to other loans.
2. The borrower must be delinquent in payments or at imminent risk of default. Loans in foreclosure or bankruptcy are eligible.
3. The borrower must document a financial hardship with a signed RMA or Hardship Affidavit.
4. The real estate must be a single-family property consisting of one to four residential units. However, there is no occupancy requirement.
5. The property must not be condemned, though it may be vacant.
6. The current loan principal balance, excluding late payments and fees, may not exceed the following limits:
   - $729,750 for one unit;
   - $934,200 for two units;
   - $1,129,250 for three units; or
   - $1,403,400 for four units.

Evaluation of HAFA Eligibility

First, the servicer must find the borrower, loan, and property eligible for HAFA. Then, evaluation begins with the RMA if income is to be considered, or with the substitute Hardship Affidavit. The servicer may use borrower information completed and verified during HAMP consideration.

[i]The Dodd–Frank Wall Street Reform and Consumer Protection Act of 2010, named for Sen. Chris Dodd and Rep. Barney Frank, involves broad Wall Street and mortgage reform. It prohibits mortgage loans to anyone convicted of such violations as fraud or money laundering. Signing a Dodd–Frank Certification affirms that the applicant has no such convictions.
[ii]The monthly mortgage payment ratio equals monthly principal, interest, taxes, insurance, and association dues divided by gross monthly income. Refer to *The ABA Consumer Guide to Mortgage Modification: How to Lower Your Payments with the Home Affordable Modification Program*, also by Dean Kackley.

If a borrower or tenant wants relocation assistance, then the borrower must submit applicable evidence of occupancy. Also, a tenant must sign the Dodd–Frank Certification, which already is included in the borrower's RMA or Hardship Affidavit. Subject to servicer and mortgage investor demands, HAFA does not require income documentation, including a tax return and the Internal Revenue Service (IRS) request for tax information Form 4506-T or 4506T-EZ.

Finally, emphasis has shifted away from traditional income-based lending criteria. Until recently, short sale approval, like good lending practice, leaned heavily on proving the borrower's financial qualifications, or in this case financial hardship. Increasingly, attention focuses on market conditions and the sale transaction. HAFA now emphasizes property value, price, and net proceeds. When conflicts arise with the parties to the sale, however, the program still defers to the servicer's authority within its mortgage investor's limits.

This can help to clarify price expectations early and to reconcile such expectations among the lender, the seller, and the listing agent. Then, the Short Sale Notice (SSN), discussed later in greater detail, sets a value. As described in its HAFA policy, during the marketing phase, the lender periodically reevaluates the property value and reconciles discrepancies. If it finds that the value has declined, then the listing price must be adjusted. On the other hand, after initially agreeing to a listing price, the lender may not insist on increasing it even if market values have risen.

Expect servicers to perform a financial analysis to predict whether the short sale serves the mortgage investor's best interests. Evaluating HAMP modifications involves a complex computer model called the Base Net Present Value (NPV) Model, which projects whether modification or foreclosure yields more benefit *for the investor* (not for the borrower). Servicers must use their own model to predict whether foreclosure yields more benefit than a short sale. So, despite using a different map, the journey still leads to the same destination: whether or not foreclosure benefits the mortgage investor more.

> **CAUTION**
>
> The lender's primary legal obligation is to the investor who owns the loan that your lender services. If you are delinquent, then the lender would not be allowed to help you in any way that might compromise the investor's interest in getting paid by you.

Listing Price

One of HAFA's principal features attempts to correct a serious weakness of traditional short sales. Uncommon in the past because of a regularly appreciating real estate market, short sales completed the listing and marketing phases before the lender became involved. Only then did lenders review the purchase agreement and decide on an acceptable value. Differences between the sale price and the lender's value led to lengthy negotiations and delays. HAFA calls for reconciliation of price and value at the listing stage.

The term "minimum acceptable net proceeds" (minimum net) means the amount a lender expects to receive from the short sale after subtracting all transaction costs.

At a borrower's request, the servicer projects results for a short sale and determines the minimum net needed to satisfy the mortgage investor's best interests. The minimum net may be expressed as a percentage of either the market value or the listing price of the property. It also may be expressed as a fixed dollar amount, to which projected expenses of the sale can be added to arrive at an acceptable price. HAFA encourages this exchange before or during the listing phase.

Whether expressed as a percentage of value or price or as a fixed amount, the minimum net accounts for transaction expenses. Such expenses include "reasonable and customary real estate transaction costs for the community" where the property is located. An experienced real estate, escrow, title, or closing agent should know what constitutes the transaction expenses. If the servicer underestimates them, then make your argument in a documented dispute or escalation. However, the final determination of expenses depends on what the servicer or investor is willing to pay.

Borrower Protections

HAFA offers borrowers several forms of protection, including limitation of postsale liability, suspension of foreclosure sale, and relocation assistance, all addressed in more detail later. Other protections prohibit passing through most sale costs to the borrower and enable a nondelinquent borrower to maintain an unblemished payment record.

NOTE

If the IRS is holding a lien on the property, it typically will issue a certificate of discharge of property (release of tax lien) in a short sale because the senior mortgage generally leaves no equity in the property—making the IRS lien valueless. Refer to Interim Guidance SBSE-05-1010-054 (October 4, 2011) and Internal Revenue Code section 6325(b)(2)(B).

From the total sale proceeds, the lender is expected to pay all fees, commissions, other charges, and out-of-pocket expenses associated with the sale. In addition, the lender pays subordinate mortgage holders a negotiated amount up to $8,500 to settle their loans, usually arranged by the borrower or the borrower's agent. Although HAFA does not require it, the lender might pay to remove other liens—property tax liens, homeowners association liens, mechanic's liens, and local or state assessments, for example.

Lenders may not require borrowers to reimburse operational, administrative, and overhead costs incurred while processing a successful short sale, although such costs may be added to the unpaid mortgage balance if the short sale fails. The servicer must arrange cooperation by a mortgage insurer, which guaranteed payment on a high-LTV loan, if one is involved. Neither may require a payment at closing or a promise to pay (promissory note) after closing by the borrower.

The agreement by a lender to allow a short sale might require the borrower to make monthly payments until the sale closes. If so, such payments may not exceed 31 percent of the borrower's monthly gross income, which might result in an amount less than the full regular monthly mortgage payment. It is possible

If a short sale fails, the various costs incurred in the process may be added to the unpaid principal balance, increasing the deficiency. Then, in a subsequent short sale or foreclosure, the potential deficiency liability will also increase.

CAUTION

for a borrower to remain current up to this point. However, making a lower payment (or no payment, if one is not required) would result in a derogatory credit report. HAFA allows a borrower to make the full contract payment to stay current and to preserve good credit standing, unless mortgage investor guidelines limit short sales to delinquent loans (borrowers).

Release of Liability

Real estate loans consist of two parts: the loan itself, evidenced by the promissory note, which contains the borrower's promise to repay the money borrowed; and, the collateral, evidenced by a written and recorded security instrument—lien, mortgage, or deed of trust—that gives the lender the right to sell the real estate if the borrower fails to repay the loan as agreed. The term "mortgage" may refer to the two parts together or to the security instrument alone. The term "lien" usually refers only to the collateral interest, which probably secures a related obligation.

Any party with an interest in the property—owner, lender, or other lien holder—must release its interest, which encumbers or limits ownership in some way, before title can pass free and clear in a sale to the buyer. However, a party releasing its interest in the property does not, in itself, release the underlying obligation. Simply said, clearing the title does not clear the loan.

Traditionally in real estate sales, the lender received the full outstanding loan balance, which satisfied the obligation, and it released or removed its lien unconditionally. In a short sale, the lender receives less than the full outstanding loan balance, which leaves a deficiency, and it releases its lien subject to the deficiency, which becomes an unsecured personal liability of the borrower.

In the past, a lender might release its security interest in the property, but it would not release the promissory note, which could be enforced by suing the borrower and obtaining a deficiency judgment. HAFA endeavors to close this gap by requiring lenders to waive their right to seek a deficiency judgment. Some states require such a waiver by statute. In California, for example, when a lender approves the short sale of a one-to-four-unit residential property, it waives by statute any right to pursue the borrower to recover the deficiency.

If others hold a financial interest in the property or a loan affected by the sale—for example, a subordinate lien, an equity loan or homeowner line of credit, a mechanic's lien, or a property or federal tax lien—the borrower is primarily responsible for obtaining their agreement to allow the sale. A junior lender may receive up to $8,500 from the sale proceeds, at the senior lender's expense, but others might receive nothing unless it is from the senior lender's benevolence.

Once the lien is satisfied, the lien holder releases the lien, which then allows the title to pass unencumbered (free and clear) to the buyer.

When a second subordinate lender agrees to the short sale, it also must agree to the short payoff and release deficiency liability. It must do so in writing. HAFA doesn't want any forgetfulness or change of heart when everybody arrives at the closing table. It should go without saying, however, that all such agreements must be in writing. Whether it's from the senior or junior lender, or it is a tax or mechanic's lien, get the release in writing. Insist on it.

Neither may a subordinate lien holder—second or junior lender or anyone else—require a contribution from the borrower *or the real estate agent* as a condition for releasing its security interest or for waiving the borrower's personal liability. This applies to reduction of a real estate commission, a cash contribution at or before closing, a promissory note or promise to pay after closing, use of relocation assistance funds, or imposition of prohibited fees.

Beware the end run. Lenders may set their minimum net (the amount they expect to receive after transaction costs) as a percent of the sale price. For example, one large lender allows 8 percent for seller closing costs. After a reasonable commission, little is left. The solution falls predictably to the real estate agents.

Suspension of Foreclosure

A servicer dealing with a borrower in default must consider that borrower for HAFA before beginning the foreclosure process. After such consideration, however, guidelines defer to the servicer's discretion. Consistent with its HAFA policy, a servicer may begin and continue foreclosure during HAFA marketing and approval. Actual sale by foreclosure is prohibited while a borrower's eligibility is being determined or a qualified short sale is being completed.

However, be aware of what can happen if the servicer does not approve the short sale. The foreclosure auction may occur at any time once five days have elapsed since the servicer sent the nonapproval notice. Because HAFA cannot interrupt the scheduling of a foreclosure—only the actual foreclosure sale—this leaves very little time. Stay in touch with your lender no matter how likely an approval seems. Likewise, stay in touch with the buyer, because a canceled sale leads very directly to a nonapproval notice.

Tenants with a legitimate lease might be able to remain through the lease term, or to insist on at least 90 days' notice to vacate a property transferred by foreclosure. Refer to Public Law No. 111-22, Helping Families Save Their Homes Act of 2009, Title VII, Sections 701–04, Protecting Tenants at Foreclosure Act of the Dodd–Frank Wall Street Reform and Consumer Protection Act.

Relocation Assistance

An occupant required to vacate a property as the result of a HAFA short sale might be entitled to receive a relocation assistance payment, formerly referred to as an incentive. The property must be the person's principal residence when the HAFA process begins. This rule applies to borrowers who sell their homes and to tenants of properties sold by their landlords. Whether for themselves or for their tenants, borrowers make the claim and submit proof of residency and a Dodd–Frank Certification.

The amount of the relocation assistance is $3,000 per transaction, regardless of the number of occupants or units. For example, if the homeowner's family must vacate the home, then the entire amount is paid to the seller. If tenants or other non-owners occupy the property, then the borrower decides on allocation of the payment. The senior lender pays the amount from the sale proceeds at closing for occupants who have already vacated or by check after occupants surrender the premises and keys. Then MHA reimburses the amount to the lender, effectively eliminating any impact on minimum net or debt forgiveness that might penalize the borrower.

A borrower who receives relocation assistance may pocket the amount or use it to pay for overdue utilities, legal expenses, minor property repairs identified during an inspection, and the like. However, borrowers may not use any of the relocation assistance funds to release a subordinate mortgage or other lien or for the lender's transaction costs.

> **CAUTION**
>
> A lender might offer more than the HAFA-required $3,000 for relocation expenses. In one example, a borrower who did not qualify for a HAMP or proprietary modification was then offered a $30,000 incentive to close a short sale rather than proceed to foreclosure. Inquire first about relocation assistance and second about short sale incentives.

Short Sale Notice

When an eligible borrower expresses interest in a short sale, the servicer determines whether the hypothetical sale serves the mortgage investor's best interests. It then preapproves a listing price or minimum net and sends to the borrower an SSN outlining the terms and conditions required for a HAFA sale. In addition to price predictability, the SSN promises at least 120 days to market and close the sale. An alternative starting point is after a purchase agreement is signed, which will be discussed later in this chapter.

The SSN gives the borrower and listing agent a stationary platform from which to market the property and accept a buyer's offer. The seller, the buyer, and their representatives may proceed on the servicer's commitment, enforceable by the seller through MHA and U.S. Treasury escalation procedures. The SSN is not a sale or purchase agreement, but it clarifies in advance what that agreement—between the borrower as seller and the buyer—must look like.

The SSN path begins when a borrower requests preapproval of a short sale, either at the borrower's initiative or in response to the servicer's solicitation. If the borrower already submitted an RMA or Hardship Affidavit, or if it has a "predetermined hardship," then the servicer must respond within 30 days, during which a foreclosure sale may not occur. A predetermined hardship means the borrower's mortgage payments are 90 days or more delinquent and the borrower's FICO score is below 620.

Otherwise, within five days, the servicer must send the borrower written confirmation of the request. The servicer must include with the written confirmation a blank Hardship Affidavit or RMA for the borrower to complete and submit, as well as a description of the HAFA evaluation process, which begins when the servicer receives the completed Hardship Affidavit or RMA.

After confirming the borrower's HAFA eligibility, the servicer performs an evaluation. It doesn't use the Base NPV Model, designed specifically for modifications, but it probably runs a similar financial analysis consistent with investor expectations. If the servicer fails to answer the borrower within 30 days, it must send a written status notice with progress updates every 15 days afterward.

The process concludes in one of three ways: (a) approval of the borrower for HAFA and preapproval of short sale terms, (b) nonapproval for HAFA but with an explanation of other proprietary short sale options, or (c) nonapproval of any short sale.

When preapproving a HAFA short sale, servicers may use the standard MHA SSN form or adapt it to investor limitations, state regulations, and local real estate practice. Nevertheless, at a minimum, the agreement must provide:

- Either a listing price or minimum net.
- A fixed termination date not less than 120 days or more than 12 months after the SSN start (SSN effective date).
- The servicer's promise not to complete a foreclosure sale during the SSN term.
- A requirement to list the property for sale with a local licensed real estate professional and for the real estate commission not to exceed 6 percent.
- That allowable closing (transaction) costs are to be deducted from the gross sale proceeds.
- That the monthly mortgage payment during the SSN term, if any, is not to exceed 31 percent of the borrower's monthly gross income.
- Notice that the borrower may choose to make full monthly payments to stay current on the loan.
- A list of documents required with the sales contract for the short sale to be approved.
- The conditions under which the SSN can be terminated.
- Clauses to be included in listing and sale agreements about servicer approval, arm's length transaction, contract cancellation, and prohibition on resale within 30 days or at a price greater than 120 percent of the HAFA price within 90 days.
- Various closing notifications, including release of the borrower from deficiency liability, availability of relocation assistance, settlement of subordinate liens from sale proceeds and release of borrower liability, and professional advice regarding income tax consequences.

Terminating the SSN

During the SSN, the servicer may terminate its preapproval due to any of the following circumstances if described in the SSN:

- The borrower experiences a significantly improved financial situation, qualifies for a modification, or brings the mortgage account current.
- The borrower or listing broker fails to act in good faith in listing, marketing, or closing the sale.
- The property condition or value changes significantly.
- The borrower files for bankruptcy or a bankruptcy court declines to approve a sale.
- Litigation is started that might interfere with valid conveyance of the property.
- The borrower fails to make monthly payments if any are required by the SSN.

While foreclosure efforts must be suspended during the SSN, failure to make a monthly payment required by the SSN terminates the suspension, and a foreclosure may proceed to sale.

During the SSN period, the borrower should provide the servicer with the listing agreement and information about subordinate liens and should begin to arrange evidence of occupancy and Dodd–Frank Certification for anyone requesting relocation assistance. The borrower and any other occupants must maintain the property in good condition and fully cooperate with the listing agent to market the property.

Approval of a Short Sale

After receiving and accepting a purchase offer, the borrower requests approval of the executed sales contract by submitting it within three business days together with other "offer documents" including:

- A copy of the signed purchase offer (sales contract) with all addenda, as well as all disclosures and related signed or initialed forms.
- Documentation regarding the buyer's funds (account statement) or loan preapproval on lender letterhead. Though not stipulated, assume that you will need proof of both down payment *and* loan preapproval.
- Information about subordinate liens, their status, and progress toward negotiating their release.

If the sales contract meets or exceeds the SSN terms and conditions, including the minimum net, the servicer must approve the sale within ten business days after receiving the offer documents. If the contract fails to meet any of the terms and conditions, including the minimum net, the servicer may approve, disapprove, or express its intention to counteroffer, which must actually happen within 30 calendar days after receiving the offer documents.

The servicer *may* approve a lower minimum net, but it may not reduce the real estate commission or require contributions by the agent or the borrower. The servicer may designate a time frame for closing, but it cannot be less than 45 days from the sales contract date unless the borrower consents.

To summarize, if SSN terms are met, the servicer must approve the purchase (sale) agreement, must allow 45 days to close (during which the occupant may stay in the property), may not reduce the real estate commission, and may not ask the real estate agent or the borrower to contribute financially.

Alternative: Start with the Sales Contract

An alternative approval process begins with a signed purchase (sale) agreement, rather than an SSN. In effect, the borrower requests approval by submitting the executed contract. I suggest that the borrower also include the following if available:

- All addenda and attachments to the executed contract.
- Hardship Affidavit or RMA.
- Documentation regarding the buyer's funds (account statement) or loan preapproval on lender letterhead. Though it is not stipulated, assume that you will need proof of both down payment and loan preapproval.
- Information about subordinate liens, their status, and progress toward negotiating their release.
- Evidence of occupancy for residents of the property, and the Dodd–Frank Certification for tenants eligible for relocation assistance.

To avoid delays at this critical transaction stage, the servicer must respond within five business days with an Acknowledgment of Request for Short Sale (ARSS). The ARSS identifies additional documentation needed and includes a Hardship Affidavit or RMA, if not already submitted by the borrower.

Within 30 calendar days after receiving the executed sales contract, the servicer determines the borrower's eligibility for HAFA, provides information about HAMP for the borrower to consider before selling, and either approves, disapproves, or conditions approval on changes to the agreement in the form of a counteroffer.

If the price minus allowable costs equals or exceeds the minimum net and if other terms and conditions of the SSN are met, the servicer *must* approve. It *may* approve a lower minimum net. Approval cannot involve reducing the real estate commission or requiring contributions by the agent or the borrower. The servicer may designate a time frame for closing, but it cannot be less than 45 days from the sales contract date unless the borrower consents.

NOTE

Rather than starting the process with an SSN, an alternative is to start with a sales contract. A potential problem with this approach is that the lender may believe the property is worth more than the price in the sales contract. So if you go this route, plan on decision and processing delays.

Most lenders will alert borrowers about incomplete submissions, but MHA guidelines give no direction, so stay in touch with the lender regarding the status of the transaction.

Deed-in-Lieu of Foreclosure

A DIL transfers property ownership to the lender rather than proceeding to foreclosure on a delinquent loan. It is sometimes referred to as "handing over the keys." HAFA leaves this option to a servicer's discretion consistent with its HAFA policy and mortgage investor guidelines. To approve a HAFA DIL, the servicer and mortgage investor must release the debt and waive related claims against the borrower. Transfer of title extinguishes the mortgage lien.

Typically, before accepting a DIL, servicers expect borrowers to make good-faith efforts to list and market a property. Under circumstances agreeable to the investor, HAFA allows servicers to accept a DIL without requiring a marketing period. Most likely, the borrower and servicer entered into an SSN that expired without a sale. If it included an optional DIL provision, the investor would be obligated to take the DIL.

Of potential interest are the following possibilities. If an owner or tenant must vacate on completion of the DIL transaction (closing), relocation assistance of $3,000 may be available. On the other hand, a servicer may allow an owner or tenant to continue occupying the property. HAFA theoretically allows lenders to accept a DIL, and then lease back (deed-for-lease) the property to the defaulting owner with or without a future buy-back option. Though only a remote possibility, such an arrangement would be included in the DIL agreement with the servicer and would be endorsed by the investor. If interested in this option, speak with a supervisor at your lender's place of business.

Short Sale versus Modification

A borrower may not participate in an SSN and an HAMP Trial Period Plan (TPP) at the same time, according to MHA guidelines. This suggests that a borrower could list and market the property without an SSN while applying for HAMP but before TPP approval.

Because MHA guidelines do not specifically endorse the approach, permission probably falls to servicer discretion. The RMA asks whether the property is for sale; if the answer is yes, it might interfere with your HAMP application. If you try this approach, be sure that your real estate broker is on board, and that the listing agreement allows for cancellation on entering a TPP.

Summary

The HAFA short sale program brings predictability to a process that has caused buyers, sellers, and their agents untold frustration and that has left too many homes in foreclosure. Initiating the HAFA process at the listing stage puts the seller and lender in agreement about price and the time required to market the property.

The price is less than the loan amount, and clarity about the lender's expectations is essential to a successful closing. The SSN serves this purpose. The lender then provides an ARSS, reviews eligibility and supporting documentation, and approves the final terms and conditions between the seller and buyer.

The SSN also effectively suspends foreclosure during a specified marketing period. Other benefits of HAFA include relocation assistance for occupants displaced by the sale, and release of the seller/borrower from personal liability for the deficiency or shortfall between the loan amount and the sale proceeds.

CHAPTER

5

Escalation

Challenging Noncompliance

Learning Points

- What should you do if you disagree with a lender's procedure or decision?
- What does escalation mean and how can you use it?
- Who can dispute the lender's findings?

Early and persistent failure by some servicers to implement the Making Home Affordable (MHA) program in good faith forced the U.S. Department of the Treasury to renew efforts aimed at correcting errors, delays, and redundancies by lenders. The process escalates disputes arising primarily from interpretation of guidelines, eligibility decisions, property valuation, notification deadlines, and human error.

Initiated by the borrower or borrower's representative, escalation begins and ends within the servicer's loss-mitigation hierarchy, subject to initiative and review by federal MHA personnel. Escalation endeavors to remedy mistakes, ironically by using the same information that led to the dispute. The servicer alleged to have made the mistake is expected to correct it. Aggrieved borrowers may advocate for themselves, or they may call upon third-party nonprofit or private counselors, according to a defined procedure.

Most importantly, the rules prohibit foreclosure sales during the escalation process. For modifications, www.CheckMyNPV.com attempts to remove some of the mystery surrounding the most common conflict, the complex net present value (NPV) test. Many short sale conflicts can be avoided by the use of a Short Sale Notice (SSN).

Resources

People inquiring about mortgage relief will hear from their lender about a free 24-hour telephone help-line operated by the nonprofit Homeownership Preservation Foundation (HPF). The HOPE™ Hotline (888-995-HOPE) directs callers to U.S. Department of Housing and Urban Development (HUD)-approved housing counselors who provide homeowners with free foreclosure prevention information. They are not employees of the HPF, the HUD, or Making Home Affordable (MHA) programs. They give borrowers a preliminary assessment of their eligibility for MHA programs, and refer them to MHA for detailed program or nonapproval questions. Collectively, these resources are called MHA Help, and borrowers access them directly.

Another resource is the HAMP Solution Center (HSC), which manages escalated cases exclusively from housing counselors, government offices, professional advisors, and other third parties acting on behalf of a borrower. Third-party escalation will be discussed further later in this chapter.

> **NOTE**
> The escalation process suspends foreclosure sales, and it is expected that the lender will correct any mistakes identified by its own personnel or federal regulators.

Escalated Cases

Borrower inquiries and disputes that rise to the level of an "escalated case" usually involve the following issues:

- Whether the servicer considered the borrower for the correct MHA program(s);
- Whether the nonapproval or the servicer's written explanation was incorrect; or
- Whether the servicer started or continued foreclosure contrary to guidelines.

An escalated case might begin in the federal hierarchy. Then, the HSC or MHA Help refers the case to the servicer.

A borrower or authorized third party initiates the case, usually after failing to solicit a satisfactory response to the issues from established loss-mitigation contacts. Whoever escalates the case is thereafter called the requestor. That term might refer to the borrower, a nonprofit housing counselor, a real estate professional, an attorney, an elected official or the official's staff, MHA Help, the HSC, or Department of Treasury personnel.

Servicers must have written procedures and adequate personnel in place to provide timely and appropriate responses to escalated cases. Hypothetically, with oversight from MHA, servicers decide the outcome, thereby correcting their own mistakes. If the loan information and other facts of an inquiry are "substantially similar" to a previously resolved case, however, the servicer may refuse to review it.

Resolution and steps to implement it are communicated within ten days to the borrower and to the requestor, if they are different entities. When HSC or MHA Help concurs with the resolution and the first implementation step occurs, the servicer closes the escalated case.

TIP

Become as knowledgeable as possible regarding your appeal and what mistakes were made by the lender. Provide the lender with full documentation, and be prepared to respond to objections from the lender.

Third-Party Escalation

The world of mortgage relief divides borrowers' representatives into for-profit private advisors and not-for-profit MHA Help counselors, government representatives, and nonprofits sometimes sanctioned by HUD. When authorized by a borrower, any of these representatives can serve as a requestor. Most servicers refer to them all as third-party advocates or representatives, and almost everybody cautions borrowers to be on guard against phonies and scams.

The following steps apply to authorized third parties as well as to borrowers advocating for themselves.

To justify opening an escalated case, introduced in the preceding section, a claim must contend that the servicer did not assess the borrower for the correct MHA program(s) or that the servicer failed to comply with program guidelines. If you believe that a servicer incorrectly interpreted MHA guidelines, take the following steps.

Step 1: If working through the usual contacts and channels at the servicer does not resolve the issue, elevate your concern by asking to speak with a senior manager. Some examples of valid reasons for Step 1 escalation arise when the servicer:

- Refuses to stop a scheduled foreclosure sale while evaluating a borrower.
- Charges up-front fees.
- Instructs the borrower to miss a payment.
- Claims that the Department of the Treasury (MHA) is causing the delay.
- Advises a borrower to intentionally misrepresent information.
- Claims nonparticipation when Fannie Mae or Freddie Mac owns your loan.
- Incorrectly denies the borrower's request.

Step 2: If Step 1 does not resolve the issue, then contact the appropriate escalation team:

- If Fannie Mae owns the loan (www.knowyouroptions.com/loanlookup), then call 1-800-7FANNIE(732-6643), or e-mail resource_center@ fanniemae.com.

- If Freddie Mac owns the loan (www.freddiemac.com/mymortgage), then call 1-800-FREDDIE(373-3343), or e-mail borrower_outreach@ freddiemac.com.
- If neither Government Sponsored Enterprises (GSE) owns the loan, then contact the HSC by phone at 1-866-939-4469 or e-mail escalations@ hmpadmin.com. Property owners should call 888-995-HOPE(4673).

Also use these contacts when a servicer incorrectly claims that its mortgage investor does not participate in HAMP—for example, if a GSE (Fannie Mae or Freddie Mac) owns the loan.

To assist a borrower, a counselor must provide written authorization from the borrower to the servicer granting permission to share the borrower's mortgage and personal financial information. Until the escalation team receives written authorization, it cannot disclose any of your information. Standard forms are available; ask the lender for them. To ensure acceptance, obtain signatures from all borrowers. Ask the lender for specific requirements or to provide its form.

The following information is usually sufficient. Also, have it at hand when contacting the servicer.

- Borrower name(s)
- Borrower identification (last four digits of the social security number)
- Property address
- Servicer name
- Servicer loan number
- Third-party name
- Third-party organization
- Third-party e-mail
- Third-party phone number
- Third-party relationship to borrower
- If applicable, the date of the most recent Notice of Acceleration, Notice of Default, or scheduled foreclosure auction

Be aware that signing the Request for Mortgage Assistance (RMA) or the MHA Hardship Affidavit authorizes your servicer to disclose personally identifiable information about eligibility, qualifications, and terms of MHA agreements. Despite the fact that the borrower has no choice when applying for an MHA program—and even though use of the released information is primarily for statistical and beneficial purposes—the authorization granted is nevertheless very broad.

Your information may be shared with related mortgage servicers, investors, and insurers of both senior and junior mortgages; the U.S. Department of the Treasury, Fannie Mae, Freddie Mac, and subcontractors in MHA-related roles; and HUD-approved mortgage counselors.

Be fully informed about the disputed issue. If it involves income and expense numbers or ratios, compare those submitted with any more current ones and confirm your calculations. If it involves property value, be ready to provide precise comparables, special characteristics, and written documentation. Prepare to overcome the servicer's assumption that it is right and you are wrong. Review the relevant chapters in this book.

Servicer Compliance

Within five business days after receiving an escalated case, the servicer must give the requestor and borrower written acknowledgement of the inquiry with a case reference, a toll-free telephone number for contacting escalation staff, and the resolution date. The resolution date, by which the servicer decides and communicates the outcome to the requestor and borrower, must be within 30 calendar days after the inquiry. However, failure to comply means only that servicers must then provide the status and update it every 15 days afterward until a resolution is reached. This requirement is more akin to a courtesy than to accountability.

Guidelines call for adequately trained staff to manage the escalation caseload. Escalation personnel at most major servicers function independently from those who first decided the borrower's eligibility and qualifications. They access relevant borrower documentation, directly reducing redundancy. They tend to be knowledgeable about program guidelines, familiar with internal procedures, and empowered with authority to achieve resolution. Borrowers and their authorized representatives are given direct access by telephone and e-mail to escalation staff.

Though requirements are written as mandatory, enforcement lacks authority and compliance depends on the lender's willingness and temperament.

Resolution

For each escalated case, escalation staff members review the information and documentation used by loss-mitigation personnel to arrive at the original disputed decision or action. To determine the accuracy of the dispute or inquiry, the analyst may review input values, obtain related property and personal information, recalculate the investor's present value return, and contact the investor directly.

If the borrower has been referred by HSC or MHA Help, then that entity must concur with the proposed resolution. The borrower or third-party advocate needs to be sufficiently familiar with guidelines to validate the outcome.

NOTE

Do not count the foreclosure date. Count back seven *business* days, not including weekends and bank holidays. Submit your case before midnight of that day: do so precisely according to your lender's escalation process; and be sure to submit it to the correct office, which might be different than where you previously submitted documentation. Check with your single-point-of-contact relationship manager for details.

Suspension of Foreclosure Sale

If a servicer receives an escalated case before midnight of the seventh business day prior to a scheduled foreclosure sale, it must suspend the sale until resolution of the case.

When nonapproval occurs less than seven business days before the scheduled foreclosure sale, escalate your dispute directly to the HSC or to MHA Help.

If not already in foreclosure, your loan may not be referred to foreclosure until the escalated case is resolved. If escalation has already begun, foreclosure proceedings may continue, but the sale may not occur. Actual cancellation of the sale usually happens only after completion of the corrective action, for example, final modification or short sale closing.

The servicer must instruct the attorney or trustee who actually conducts the foreclosure process to postpone it. This might occur well in advance, but often it happens within days or hours before the scheduled sale. Each postponement adds an expense, and some lenders refuse to incur the expense until the last minute. Excessive caseloads also delay postponements, adding stress to an already difficult situation.

At this end-stage of foreclosure proceedings, communicate with both the lender and the attorney or trustee conducting the foreclosure. Ensure that instructions not only have been given but have been received. Otherwise, an unexpected and unwarranted sale might mistakenly take place.

To repeat, so long as an escalated case remains unresolved, the lender may not conduct a foreclosure sale. Nor may a foreclosure conclude while an SSN is active.

If "resolution" brings no change, but your circumstances or the circumstances of your sale change, then communicate immediately with your single-point-of-contact relationship manager. Support your case with documentation. If the transaction fails, then revive a backup offer or describe the strategy that you and your real estate agent will use to expedite another offer.

It's easy to become discouraged under such pressure and stress. However, persistence can pay off. After nonapproval, many of my clients have escalated or reapplied while under the threat of foreclosure. By responding to every request on time and maintaining a current and complete application file, these clients saw scheduled foreclosure sales repeatedly postponed, resulting finally in successful sales.

Summary

Lenders make mistakes. Escalation is the process by which lenders correct their mistakes. Sellers/borrowers or their representatives initiate escalation. Although escalation cases are usually begun inside the lender's loss-mitigation hierarchy, pursue them further with the MHA organization when necessary. Though not available directly to buyers, properties can be sold through a cooperative listing agent.

In most cases, lenders do not complete foreclosure while an escalated dispute remains unresolved. However, it is essential for borrowers to maintain a complete file and to strictly comply with the lender's requirements.

6

Consequences

Learning Points

- How can you avoid deficiency liability?
- What should be considered in regard to debt forgiveness tax and exemptions?
- What is the impact of a short sale on credit reporting?

Whatever your desired course, if you are in default, attention to deficiency liability, tax liability, and credit reporting will improve your outcome. Much applies generally to all Making Home Affordable (MHA) programs. Most specifics draw from Home Affordable Modification Program (HAMP) guidance, which underlies other MHA programs like Home Affordable Foreclosure Alternatives (HAFA). Otherwise, I've relied on universal legal concepts but with some reference to California, where I practice.

Deficiency Liability

Your home or rental property serves as collateral for your real estate loan. You pledged it by giving a security interest to your lender with the right to foreclose if you defaulted on your loan payments. When a loan is not paid in full—short sale, deed-in-lieu, or foreclosure—a deficiency results. Then, when the title passes to someone else and you no longer own the property, it no longer secures the loan, and any deficiency becomes a personal obligation.

Try to avoid such an outcome. When the property transfers voluntarily in a short sale or by tender of a deed-in-lieu of foreclosure (DIL), the lender must consent by releasing its security interest. Terms and conditions are negotiable. Ensure that the lender's consent includes a release of liability and a waiver of its right to seek recovery of the deficiency from you personally. If the lender won't agree, then get professional advice and consider withdrawing from the transaction and letting the property go to foreclosure.

Ultimately, to collect, the lender would sue the borrower for the deficiency amount. If the lender wins, then the court enters a deficiency judgment, which may be enforced as any other award of the court. Your state foreclosure statutes might release you from deficiency liability by law, or they might prohibit the foreclosing lender from commencing a separate lawsuit. State laws vary. Get competent legal advice in the jurisdiction where your property is located.

If your lender refuses to release you from your deficiency liability, seek professional advice and appeal the decision. Otherwise, you may want to consider foreclosure.

Some states, like California, restrict the lender to a "single action," meaning the choice to foreclose is the single or only legal shot at the borrower and any further obligation on the borrower's part is extinguished. Because a short sale or deed-in-lieu is negotiated, the single action remains, allowing any available collection activities, including a lawsuit, to take place.

Tax Liability

If a lender waives the short sale deficiency or state law extinguishes it, that portion of the debt is forgiven and is subject to income taxation. The amount of the canceled debt must be reported as income unless one of the exceptions or exclusions described later applies. Tax liability can be an unexpected consequence, the shadow trailing behind a sense of relief and a new beginning.

The following comes directly from the identified Internal Revenue Service (IRS) publications, available through the IRS or at www.MortgageBriefing.com. It is general guidance only. **It is not tax or legal advice. Do not rely** solely on what is written here or elsewhere in this book when making decisions that might affect your federal, state, or local income tax or other taxes. State and local laws may differ from federal laws and IRS regulations, and they might impose additional taxes on debt forgiveness. Consult your professional financial, tax, or legal advisor.

The exemption expired December 31, 2012, and was extended by Congress through 2013. At this writing, extension through 2014 or beyond is pending further congressional approval.

Principal Residence Exemption

Normally, forgiven debt results in taxable income. Certain qualified debt that is reduced by mortgage restructuring (principal reduction by modification), or that is forgiven in connection with a foreclosure (short sale or DIL) might be excluded. Source: The Mortgage Forgiveness Debt Relief Act of 2007.

Qualified Debt Exemption

Qualified debt is debt that (1) was used to buy, build, or substantially improve the taxpayer's principal residence; (2) was secured by that residence; and (3) did not exceed $2 million (or $1 million for a married person filing a separate return). Debt used to refinance qualified debt is also eligible for the exclusion, but only up to the amount of the old mortgage principal, just before the refinancing. (Cash-out or equity loans, therefore, would not qualify.) Source: IRS Publication 4705, Mortgage Forgiveness. For more information, see also IRS Publication 523, Selling Your Home.

Debt Forgiveness Exemption

Borrowers whose debt is reduced or eliminated receive a year-end statement (IRS Form 1099-C) from their lender. Lenders are required to furnish this form to borrowers by January 31. By law, this form must show the amount of debt forgiven and the fair market value of any property relinquished through foreclosure. (Refer disputes to your lender and, for HAFA, to the HAMP Solution Center [HSC].) In most cases, eligible homeowners need to report the amount; then, for the exemption, they must complete and attach IRS Form 982, Reduction of Tax Attributes Due to Discharge of Indebtedness.

Insolvency

Debt forgiven on second homes, rental property, business property, credit cards, or car loans does not qualify for the homeowner tax-relief exemption. In some cases, however, other kinds of tax relief (based on insolvency for example) may be available. Source: IRS Publication 4705, Mortgage Forgiveness.

Do not include canceled debt in reported income to the extent that you were insolvent immediately before the cancellation. Source: IRS Publication 4681, Canceled Debts, Foreclosures, Repossessions, and Abandonments—for individuals, 2008 returns.

Here, "insolvent" means that the total of all your liabilities exceeded the fair market value (FMV) of all your assets, meaning the value of everything you own. This includes assets that serve as collateral for debt. It includes exempt assets, which are beyond the reach of your creditors under the law, such as your interest in a pension plan and the value of your retirement account. Source: IRS Publication 4681.

Liabilities include the entire amount of recourse (personal) debts, and the amount of nonrecourse (secured) debt that does not exceed the FMV of the property securing such debt. Excluded are debts discharged in Title 11 bankruptcy, and qualified principal residence indebtedness (see the earlier discussion under the heading "Principle Residence Exemption"). Source: IRS Publication 4681.

However, the liability is limited to the market value of the underwater property, so the loan amount exceeding the value could not offset the value of other

If your primary asset is an underwater home, and you have a car loan or lease and credit card balances, then you might be "insolvent" by IRS standards, despite making ends meet.

assets. Also keep in mind that if the deficiency has not been forgiven, then there is no debt forgiveness tax liability.

Generally, if you exclude canceled debt from income under one of these provisions, you must also reduce your tax attributes (certain credits, losses, and basis of assets). Consult your tax advisor. Source: IRS Publication 4681.

Bankruptcy

Debt canceled in a Title 11 bankruptcy case is not included in your income. Source: IRS Publication 4681.

Credit Reporting

Credit reporting for short sales falls into one of two categories, depending on whether the lender forgives the deficiency. When the deficiency is forgiven, the lender reports the loan as "paid in full for less than the full balance." Translation: Although it was less than the full remaining loan balance at the time of the short sale, the minimum net was accepted by the lender in full satisfaction of the debt. The report shows the account to be closed with a zero balance and nothing past due. It ends any further reporting on the loan.

When the deficiency is not forgiven, the lender reports the account as "collateral released by creditor with balance owing." Translation: The lender released the lien so clear title could pass to the short sale buyer, but it did not waive the deficiency liability. The report continues to show an open account with the same loan, the same account number, and the same original loan amount and date.

Going forward, the lender reports account activity as for any other credit account. The short sale reduced the outstanding balance by the amount of the net sale price, resulting in a new balance equal to the deficiency amount. Other changes depend on agreement between lender and borrower. They might include extending the loan term duration, changing the monthly payment, or forbearing payments or interest for a period of time. The lender reports the original or changed terms, and it reports on-time payments as current or late payments as delinquent. Reporting on the account continues until it is paid in full or moved to another status, such as charged off, discharged in bankruptcy, or subject to a deficiency judgment.

In either case, whether the deficiency is waived or not, any derogatory reports for late payments before closing the short sale will remain on the borrower's credit record.

Needless to say, an open deficiency poses ongoing liability and credit difficulties. A foreclosure might offer an alternative that brings a conclusion to the account and a foundation for healing credit. If the primary senior lender refuses to waive deficiency liability in a short sale, consider canceling the sale and proceeding to foreclosure. Your decision should take into consideration the foreclosure laws in your state and possible nonextinguishment of a second loan, if any.

Summary

Before closing a short sale, check for release from deficiency liability, anticipate debt forgiveness tax and possible exemptions, and learn about credit reporting. In extreme cases, consider canceling the sale and enduring foreclosure. Get professional legal and tax advice, and consider both federal and state laws and taxes.

CHAPTER

7

Conclusion

A final word about mortgage relief and the consequences of a short sale: Consider more than the liability and credit advantages. Many of my clients initiated a solution to an overwhelming and self-defeating problem, whether it was an unaffordable mortgage or an underwater loan or both.

Some wanted to stay and spent months of anxiety and aggravation feeding the modification monster, only to run out of time, patience, and energy. Others turned directly to a short sale as the solution of choice. Either way, these clients have something in common.

They did what property owners do when it's time to leave. They sold. They didn't walk away. They endured a little more pain, regained their sense of self worth, and began to heal mentally, emotionally, and financially.

I recommend it.

The forms in this section are included only for general reference and are not intended for reproduction or submission purposes. MHA forms can be found using the "Borrower Documents" tab at https://www.hmpadmin.com/portal/programs/foreclosure_alternatives.jsp.

APPENDIX

A

Request for Mortgage Assistance

Making Home Affordable Program
Request For Mortgage Assistance (RMA)

If you are experiencing a financial hardship and need help, you must complete and submit this form along with other required documentation to be considered for foreclosure prevention options under the Making Home Affordable (MHA) Program. You must provide information about yourself and your intentions to either keep or transition out of your property; a description of the hardship that prevents you from paying your mortgage(s); information about **all** of your income, expenses and financial assets; whether you have declared bankruptcy; and information about the mortgage(s) on your principal residence and other single family real estate that you own. Finally, you will need to return to your loan servicer (1) this completed, signed and dated Request for Mortgage Assistance (RMA); and (2) completed and signed IRS Form 4506-T or 4506T-EZ; and (3) all required income documentation identified in Section 4.

When you sign and date this form, you will make important certifications, representations and agreements, including certifying that all of the information in this RMA is accurate and truthful.

SECTION 1: BORROWER INFORMATION

BORROWER	CO-BORROWER
BORROWER'S NAME	CO-BORROWER'S NAME
SOCIAL SECURITY NUMBER DATE OF BIRTH (MM/DD/YY)	SOCIAL SECURITY NUMBER DATE OF BIRTH (MM/DD/YY)
HOME PHONE NUMBER WITH AREA CODE	HOME PHONE NUMBER WITH AREA CODE
CELL OR WORK NUMBER WITH AREA CODE	CELL OR WORK NUMBER WITH AREA CODE
MAILING ADDRESS	MAILING ADDRESS (IF SAME AS BORROWER, WRITE "SAME")
EMAIL ADDRESS	EMAIL ADDRESS

Has any borrower filed for bankruptcy? ☐ Chapter 7 ☐ Chapter 13	Is any borrower a servicemember? ☐ Yes ☐ No
Filing Date: _____ Bankruptcy case number: _____	Have you recently been deployed away from your principal residence or recently received a permanent change of station order? ☐ Yes ☐ No
Has your bankruptcy been discharged? ☐ Yes ☐ No	

How many single family properties other than your principal residence do you and/or any co-borrower(s) own individually, jointly, or with others? _____

Has the mortgage on your principal residence ever had a Home Affordable Modification Program (HAMP) trial period plan or permanent modification? ☐ Yes ☐ No

Has the mortgage on any other property that you or any co-borrower own had a permanent HAMP modification? ☐ Yes ☐ No   If "Yes", how many? _____

Are you or any co-borrower currently in or being considered for a HAMP trial period plan on a property other than your principal residence? ☐ Yes ☐ No

SECTION 2: HARDSHIP AFFIDAVIT

I (We) am/are requesting review under MHA
I am having difficulty making my monthly payment because of financial difficulties created by (check all that apply):

☐	My household income has been reduced. For example: reduced pay or hours, decline in business or self employment earnings, death, disability or divorce of a borrower or co-borrower.	☐	My monthly debt payments are excessive and I am overextended with my creditors. Debt includes credit cards, home equity or other debt.
☐	My expenses have increased. For example: monthly mortgage payment reset, high medical or health care costs, uninsured losses, increased utilities or property taxes.	☐	My cash reserves, including all liquid assets, are insufficient to maintain my current mortgage payment and cover basic living expenses at the same time.
☐	I am unemployed and (a) I am receiving/will receive unemployment benefits or (b) my unemployment benefits ended less than 6 months ago.	Other:	

Explanation (continue on a separate sheet of paper if necessary):

SECTION 3: PRINCIPAL RESIDENCE INFORMATION
(This section is required even if you are not seeking mortgage assistance on your principal residence)

I am requesting mortgage assistance with my principal residence ☐ Yes ☐ No

If "yes", I want to: ☐ Keep the property ☐ Sell the property

Property Address: _____ Loan I.D. Number: _____

Other mortgages or liens on the property? ☐ Yes ☐ No Lien Holder / Servicer Name: _____ Loan I.D. Number: _____

Do you have condominium or homeowner association (HOA) fees? ☐ Yes ☐ No If "Yes", Monthly Fee $_____ Are fees paid current? ☐ Yes ☐ No

Name and address that fees are paid to: _____

Does your mortgage payment include taxes and Insurance? ☐ Yes ☐ No If "No", are the taxes and insurance paid current? ☐ Yes ☐ No

Annual Homeowner's Insurance $_____

Is the property listed for sale? ☐ Yes ☐ No If "Yes", Listing Agent's Name: _____ Phone Number: _____

List date? _____ Have you received a purchase offer? ☐ Yes ☐ No Amount of Offer $_____ Closing Date: _____

Complete this section ONLY if you are requesting mortgage assistance with a property that is not your principal residence.

Principal residence servicer name: _____ Principal residence servicer phone number: _____

Is the mortgage on your principal residence paid? ☐ Yes ☐ No if "No", number of months your payment is past due (if known): _____

SECTION 4: COMBINED INCOME AND EXPENSE OF BORROWER AND CO-BORROWER

Monthly Household Income		Monthly Household Expenses/Debt (*Principal Residence Expense Only)		Household Assets	
Monthly Gross wages	$	First Mortgage Principal & Interest Payment*	$	Checking Account(s)	$
Overtime	$	Second Mortgage Principal & Interest Payment*	$	Checking Account(s)	$
Self employment Income	$	Homeowner's Insurance*	$	Savings / Money Market	$
Unemployment Income	$	Property Taxes*	$	CDs	$
Untaxed Social Security / SSD	$	HOA/Condo Fees*	$	Stocks / Bonds	$
Food Stamps/Welfare	$	Credit Cards/Installment debt (total min. payment)	$	Other Cash on Hand	$
Taxable Social Security or retirement income	$	Child Support / Alimony	$		
Child Support / Alimony**	$	Car Payments	$		
Tips, commissions, bonus and overtime	$	Mortgage Payments other properties****	$		
Gross Rents Received ***	$	Other	$	Value of all Real Estate except principal residence	$
Other	$			Other	$
Total (Gross Income)	$	Total Debt/Expenses	$	Total Assets	$

** Alimony, child support or separate maintenance income need not be disclosed if you do not choose to have it considered for repaying your mortgage debt.
*** Include rental income received from all properties you own EXCEPT a property for which you are seeking mortgage assistance in Section 6.
**** Include mortgage payments on all properties you own EXCEPT your principal residence and the property for which you are seeking mortgage assistance in Section 6.

03/30/2012

Required Income Documentation (Your servicer may request additional documentation to complete your evaluation for MHA)	
All Borrowers	☐ Include a signed IRS Form 4506-T or 4506T-EZ
☐ Do you earn a wage? Borrower Hire Date (MM/DD/YY) _____ Co-borrower Hire Date (MM/DD/YY)_____	☐ For each borrower who is a salaried employee or hourly wage earner, provide the most recent pay stub(s) that reflects at least 30 days of year-to-date income.
☐ Are you self-employed?	☐ Provide your most recent signed and dated quarterly or year-to date profit and loss statement.
☐ Do you receive tips, commissions, bonuses, housing allowance or overtime?	☐ Describe the type of income, how frequently you receive the income and third party documentation describing the income (e.g., employment contracts or printouts documenting tip income).
☐ Do you receive social security, disability, death benefits, pension, public assistance or adoption assistance?	☐ Provide documentation showing the amount and frequency of the benefits, such as letters, exhibits, disability policy or benefits statement from the provider and receipt of payment (such as two most recent bank statements or deposit advices).
☐ Do you receive alimony, child support, or separation maintenance payments?	☐ Provide a copy of the divorce decree, separation agreement, or other written legal agreement filed with the court that states the amount of the payments and the period of time that you are entitled to receive them. AND ☐ Copies of your two most recent bank statements or deposit advices showing you have received payment. **Notice: Alimony, child support or separate maintenance income need not be disclosed if you do not choose to have it considered for repaying your mortgage debt.**
☐ Do you have income from rental properties that are not your principal residence?	☐ Provide your most recent Federal Tax return with all schedules, including Schedule E. ☐ If rental income is not reported on Schedule E, provide a copy of the current lease agreement with bank statements showing deposit of rent checks.

SECTION 5: OTHER PROPERTIES OWNED
(You must provide information about all properties that you or the co-borrower own, other than your principal residence and any property described in Section 6 below. Use additional sheets if necessary.)

Other Property #1

Property Address: _____ Loan I.D. Number: _____

Servicer Name: _____ Mortgage Balance $ _____ Current Value $ _____

Property is: ☐ Vacant ☐ Second or seasonal home ☐ Rented Gross Monthly Rent $ _____ Monthly mortgage payment* $ _____

Other Property #2

Property Address: _____ Loan I.D. Number: _____

Servicer Name: _____ Mortgage Balance $ _____ Current Value $ _____

Property is: ☐ Vacant ☐ Second or seasonal home ☐ Rented Gross Monthly Rent $ _____ Monthly mortgage payment* $ _____

Other Property #3

Property Address: _____ Loan I.D. Number: _____

Servicer Name: _____ Mortgage Balance $ _____ Current Value $ _____

Property is: ☐ Vacant ☐ Second or seasonal home ☐ Rented Gross Monthly Rent $ _____ Monthly mortgage payment* $ _____

* The amount of the monthly payment made to your lender – including, if applicable, monthly principal, interest, real property taxes and insurance premiums..

SECTION 6: OTHER PROPERTY FOR WHICH ASSISTANCE IS REQUESTED
(Complete this section ONLY if you are requesting mortgage assistance with a property that is not your principal residence.)

I am requesting mortgage assistance with a rental property . ☐ Yes ☐ No

I am requesting mortgage assistance with a second or seasonal home . ☐ Yes ☐ No

If "Yes" to either, I want to: ☐ Keep the property ☐ Sell the property

Property Address: _____ Loan I.D. Number: _____

Do you have a second mortgage on the property ☐ Yes ☐ No   If "Yes", Servicer Name: _____   Loan I.D. Number: _____

Do you have condominium or homeowner association (HOA) fees? ☐ Yes ☐ No   If "Yes", Monthly Fee $_____   Are HOA fees paid current? ☐ Yes ☐ No

Name and address that fees are paid to: _____

Does your mortgage payment include taxes and insurance? ☐ Yes ☐ No   If "No", are the taxes and insurance paid current? ☐ Yes ☐ No

Annual Homeowner's Insurance $_____   Annual Property Taxes $_____

If requesting assistance with a rental property, property is currently:
☐ Vacant and available for rent.
☐ Occupied without rent by your legal dependent, parent or grandparent as their principal residence.
☐ Occupied by a tenant as their principal residence.
☐ Other _____

If rental property is occupied by a tenant: Term of lease / occupancy ___/___/___ -- ___/___/___   Gross Monthly Rent $_____
MM / DD / YYYY   MM / DD / YYYY

If rental property is vacant, describe efforts to rent property: _____

If applicable, describe relationship of and duration of non-rent paying occupant of rental property: _____

Is the property for sale? ☐ Yes ☐ No   If "Yes", Listing Agent's Name: _____   Phone Number: _____

List date? _____   Have you received a purchase offer? ☐ Yes ☐ No   Amount of Offer $_____   Closing Date: _____

RENTAL PROPERTY CERTIFICATION
(You must complete this certification if you are requesting a mortgage modification with respect to a rental property.)

☐ By checking this box and initialing below, I am requesting a mortgage modification under MHA with respect to the rental property described in this Section 6 and I hereby certify under penalty of perjury that each of the following statements is true and correct with respect to that property:

1. I intend to rent the property to a tenant or tenants for at least five years following the effective date of my mortgage modification. I understand that the servicer, the U.S. Department of the Treasury, or their respective agents may ask me to provide evidence of my intention to rent the property during such time. I further understand that such evidence must show that I used reasonable efforts to rent the property to a tenant or tenants on a year-round basis, if the property is or becomes vacant during such five-year period.

   Note: The term "reasonable efforts" includes, without limitation, advertising the property for rent in local newspapers, websites or other commonly used forms of written or electronic media, and/or engaging a real estate or other professional to assist in renting the property, in either case, at or below market rent.

2. The property is not my secondary residence and I do not intend to use the property as a secondary residence for at least five years following the effective date of my mortgage modification. I understand that if I do use the property as a secondary residence during such five-year period, my use of the property may be considered to be inconsistent with the certifications I have made herein.

   Note: The term "secondary residence" includes, without limitation, a second home, vacation home or other type of residence that I personally use or occupy on a part-time, seasonal or other basis.

3. I do not own more than five (5) single-family homes (i.e, one-to-four unit properties) (exclusive of my principal residence).

Notwithstanding the foregoing certifications, I may at any time sell the property, occupy it as my principal residence, or permit my legal dependent, parent or grandparent to occupy it as their principal residence with no rent charged or collected, none of which will be considered to be inconsistent with the certifications made herein.

This certification is effective on the earlier of the date listed below or the date the RMA is received by your servicer.

Initials: Borrower _____   Co-borrower _____

03/30/2012

SECTION 7: DODD-FRANK CERTIFICATION

The following information is requested by the federal government in accordance with the Dodd-Frank Wall Street Reform and Consumer Protection Act (Pub. L. 111-203). **You are required to furnish this information.** The law provides that no person shall be eligible to begin receiving assistance from the Making Home Affordable Program, authorized under the Emergency Economic Stabilization Act of 2008 (12 U.S.C. 5201 et seq.), or any other mortgage assistance program authorized or funded by that Act, if such person, in connection with a mortgage or real estate transaction, has been convicted, within the last 10 years, of any one of the following: (A) felony larceny, theft, fraud, or forgery, (B) money laundering or (C) tax evasion.

I/we certify under penalty of perjury that I/we have not been convicted within the last 10 years of any one of the following in connection with a mortgage or real estate transaction:

    (a) felony larceny, theft, fraud, or forgery,
    (b) money laundering or
    (c) tax evasion.

I/we understand that the servicer, the U.S. Department of the Treasury, or their respective agents may investigate the accuracy of my statements by performing routine background checks, including automated searches of federal, state and county databases, to confirm that I/we have not been convicted of such crimes. I/we also understand that knowingly submitting false information may violate Federal law. This certification is effective on the earlier of the date listed below or the date this RMA is received by your servicer.

SECTION 8: INFORMATION FOR GOVERNMENT MONITORING PURPOSES

The following information is requested by the federal government in order to monitor compliance with federal statutes that prohibit discrimination in housing. **You are not required to furnish this information, but are encouraged to do so.** The law provides that a lender or servicer may not discriminate either on the basis of this information, or on whether you choose to furnish it. If you furnish the information, please provide both ethnicity and race. For race, you may check more than one designation. If you do not furnish ethnicity, race, or sex, the lender or servicer is required to note the information on the basis of visual observation or surname if you have made this request for a loan modification in person. **If you do not wish to furnish the information, please check the box below.**

BORROWER ☐ I do not wish to furnish this information   CO-BORROWER ☐ I do not wish to furnish this information

Ethnicity: ☐ Hispanic or Latino / ☐ Not Hispanic or Latino
Race: ☐ American Indian or Alaska Native / ☐ Asian / ☐ Black or African American / ☐ Native Hawaiian or Other Pacific Islander / ☐ White
Sex: ☐ Female / ☐ Male

Ethnicity: ☐ Hispanic or Latino / ☐ Not Hispanic or Latino
Race: ☐ American Indian or Alaska Native / ☐ Asian / ☐ Black or African American / ☐ Native Hawaiian or Other Pacific Islander / ☐ White
Sex: ☐ Female / ☐ Male

To be completed by Interviewer	Name/Address of Interviewer's Employer
This request was taken by: ☐ Face-to-face Interview ☐ Mail ☐ Telephone ☐ Internet	Interviewer's Name (print or type) & ID Number / Interviewer's Signature Date / Interviewer's Phone Number (include area code)	

SECTION 9: BORROWER AND CO-BORROWER ACKNOWLEDGEMENT AND AGREEMENT

1. I certify that all of the information in this RMA is truthful and the hardship(s) identified above has contributed to submission of this request for mortgage relief.

2. I understand and acknowledge that the Servicer, the U.S. Department of the Treasury, the owner or guarantor of my mortgage loan, or their respective agents may investigate the accuracy of my statements, may require me to provide additional supporting documentation and that knowingly submitting false information may violate Federal and other applicable law.

3. I authorize and give permission to the Servicer, the U.S. Department of the Treasury, and their respective agents, to assemble and use a current consumer report on all borrowers obligated on the loan, to investigate each borrower's eligibility for MHA and the accuracy of my statements and any documentation that I provide in connection with my request for assistance. I understand that these consumer reports may include, without limitation, a credit report, and be assembled and used at any point during the application process to assess each borrower's eligibility thereafter.

4. I understand that if I have intentionally defaulted on my existing mortgage, engaged in fraud or if it is determined that any of my statements or any information contained in the documentation that I provide are materially false and that I was ineligible for assistance under MHA, the Servicer, the U.S. Department of the Treasury, or their respective agents may terminate my participation in MHA, including any right to future benefits and incentives that otherwise would have been available under the program, and also may seek other remedies available at law and in equity, such as recouping any benefits or incentives previously received.

5. I certify that any property for which I am requesting assistance is a habitable residential property that is not subject to a condemnation notice.

6. I certify that I am willing to provide all requested documents and to respond to all Servicer communications in a timely manner. I understand that time is of the essence.

7. I understand that the Servicer will use the information I provide to evaluate my eligibility for available relief options and foreclosure alternatives, but the Servicer is not obligated to offer me assistance based solely on the representations in this document or other documentation submitted in connection with my request.

8. I am willing to commit to credit counseling if it is determined that my financial hardship is related to excessive debt.

9. If I am eligible for assistance under MHA, and I accept and agree to all terms of an MHA notice, plan, or agreement, I also agree that the terms of this Acknowledgment and Agreement are incorporated into such notice, plan, or agreement by reference as if set forth therein in full. My first timely payment, if required, following my servicer's determination and notification of my eligibility or prequalification for MHA assistance will serve as my acceptance of the terms set forth in the notice, plan, or agreement sent to me.

10. I understand that my Servicer will collect and record personal information that I submit in this RMA and during the evaluation process, including, but not limited to, my name, address, telephone number, social security number, credit score, income, payment history, government monitoring information, and information about my account balances and activity. I understand and consent to the Servicer's disclosure of my personal information and the terms of any MHA notice, plan or agreement to the U.S. Department of the Treasury and its agents, Fannie Mae and Freddie Mac in connection with their responsibilities under MHA, companies that perform support services in conjunction with MHA, any investor, insurer, guarantor, or servicer that owns, insures, guarantees, or services my first lien or subordinate lien (if applicable) mortgage loan(s) and to any HUD-certified housing counselor.

11. I consent to being contacted concerning this request for mortgage assistance at any e-mail address or cellular or mobile telephone number I have provided to the Servicer. This includes text messages and telephone calls to my cellular or mobile telephone.

The undersigned certifies under penalty of perjury that all statements in this document are true and correct.

_____	_____	_____	_____
Borrower Signature	Social Security Number	Date of Birth	Date
_____	_____	_____	_____
Co-borrower Signature	Social Security Number	Date of Birth	Date

03/30/2012

HOMEOWNER'S HOTLINE

If you have questions about this document or the Making Home Affordable Program, please call your servicer.
If you have questions about the program that your servicer cannot answer or need further counseling, you can call the Homeowner's HOPE™ Hotline at 1-888-995-HOPE (4673).

The Hotline can help with questions about the program and offers free HUD-certified counseling services in English and Spanish.

NOTICE TO BORROWERS

Be advised that by signing this document you understand that any documents and information you submit to your servicer in connection with the Making Home Affordable Program are under penalty of perjury. Any misstatement of material fact made in the completion of these documents including but not limited to misstatement regarding your occupancy of your property, hardship circumstances, and/or income, expenses, or assets will subject you to potential criminal investigation and prosecution for the following crimes: perjury, false statements, mail fraud, and wire fraud. The information contained in these documents is subject to examination and verification. Any potential misrepresentation will be referred to the appropriate law enforcement authority for investigation and prosecution. By signing this document you certify, represent and agree that: "Under penalty of perjury, all documents and information I have provided to my Servicer in connection with the Making Home Affordable Program, including the documents and information regarding my eligibility for the program, are true and correct."

If you are aware of fraud, waste, abuse, mismanagement or misrepresentations affiliated with the Troubled Asset Relief Program, please contact the SIGTARP Hotline by calling 1-877-SIG-2009 (toll-free), 202-622-4559 (fax), or www.sigtarp.gov and provide them with your name, our name as your servicer, your property address, loan number and the reason for escalation. Mail can be sent to Hotline Office of the Special Inspector General for Troubled Asset Relief Program, 1801 L St. NW, Washington, DC 20220.

Beware of Foreclosure Rescue Scams. Help is FREE!

- **There is never a fee to get assistance or information about the Making Home Affordable Program from your lender or a HUD-approved housing counselor.**
- **Beware of any person or organization that asks you to pay a fee in exchange for housing counseling services or modification of a delinquent loan.**
- **Beware of anyone who says they can "save" your home if you sign or transfer over the deed to your house. Do not sign over the deed to your property to any organization or individual unless you are working directly with your mortgage company to forgive your debt.**
- **Never make your mortgage payments to anyone other than your mortgage company without their approval.**

03/30/2012

APPENDIX

B

Hardship Affidavit

Making Home Affordable Program
Hardship Affidavit

MAKING HOME AFFORDABLE.GOV

HARDSHIP AFFIDAVIT page 1 | **COMPLETE ALL THREE PAGES OF THIS FORM**

▶ Loan I.D. Number_____ ▶ Servicer _____

BORROWER	CO-BORROWER
Borrower's name	Co-borrower's name
Social Security Number	Social Security Number

Property address (include city, state and zip):

I want to:	☐ Keep the Property	☐ Sell the Property	
The property is my:	☐ Principal Residence	☐ Second Home / Seasonal Rental	☐ Year-Round Rental
The property is:	☐ Owner Occupied	☐ Tenant Occupied	☐ Vacant ☐ Other _____

HARDSHIP AFFIDAVIT

I (We) am/are requesting review under the Making Home Affordable (MHA) Program.
I am having difficulty making my monthly payment because of financial difficulties created by (check all that apply):

☐ My household income has been reduced. For example: reduced pay or hours, decline in business earnings, death, disability or divorce of a borrower or co-borrower.

☐ My monthly debt payments are excessive and I am overextended with my creditors. Debt includes credit cards, home equity or other debt.

☐ My expenses have increased. For example: monthly mortgage payment reset, high medical or health care costs, uninsured losses, increased utilities or property taxes.

☐ My cash reserves, including all liquid assets, are insufficient to maintain my current mortgage payment and cover basic living expenses at the same time.

☐ I am unemployed and (a) I am receiving/will receive unemployment benefits or (b) my unemployment benefits ended less than 6 months ago.

☐ Other:

Explanation (continue on back of page 3 if necessary): _____

Have you filed for bankruptcy? ☐Yes ☐No   If yes: ☐ Chapter 7 ☐ Chapter 13   *Filing Date:*_____
Has your bankruptcy been discharged? ☐Yes ☐No   *Bankruptcy case number* _____

How many single-family properties, other than your personal residence, do you and/or your co-borrower(s) own individually, jointly, or with others? _____

Has the mortgage on your principle residence ever had a Home Affordable Modification Program (HAMP) trial-period plan or permanent modification?   ☐ Yes ☐ No

Has the mortgage or any other property that you or any co-borrower own had a permanent HAMP modification? ☐ Yes ☐ No
If "Yes", how many? _____

DODD-FRANK CERTIFICATION

The following information is requested by the federal government in accordance with the Dodd-Frank Wall Street Reform and Consumer Protection Act (Pub. L. 111-203). **You are required to furnish this information.** The law provides that no person shall be eligible to begin receiving assistance from the Making Home Affordable Program, authorized under the Emergency Economic Stabilization Act of 2008 (12 U.S.C. 5201 et seq.), or any other mortgage assistance program authorized or funded by that Act, if such person, in connection with a mortgage or real estate transaction, has been convicted, within the last 10 years, of any one of the following: (A) felony larceny, theft, fraud, or forgery, (B) money laundering or (C) tax evasion.

I/we certify under penalty of perjury that I/we have not been convicted within the last 10 years of any one of the following in connection with a mortgage or real estate transaction:

(a) felony larceny, theft, fraud, or forgery,
(b) money laundering or
(c) tax evasion.

I/we understand that the servicer, the U.S. Department of the Treasury, or their respective agents may investigate the accuracy of my statements by performing routine background checks, including automated searches of federal, state and county databases, to confirm that I/we have not been convicted of such crimes. I/we also understand that knowingly submitting false information may violate Federal law.

This certification is effective on the earlier of the date listed below or the date this hardship affidavit is received by your servicer.

RENTAL PROPERTY CERTIFICATION

You must complete this certification if you are requesting a mortgage modification with respect to a rental property.

☐ By checking this box and initialing below, I am requesting a mortgage modification under MHA with respect to the rental property having the address set forth above and I hereby certify under penalty of perjury that each of the following statements is true and correct with respect to that property:

1. I intend to rent the property to a tenant or tenants for at least five years following the effective date of my mortgage modification. I understand that the servicer, the U.S. Department of the Treasury, or their respective agents may ask me to provide evidence of my intention to rent the property during such time. I further understand that such evidence must show that I used reasonable efforts to rent the property to a tenant or tenants on a year-round basis, if the property is or becomes vacant during such five-year period.

Note: The term "reasonable efforts" includes, without limitation, advertising the property for rent in local newspapers, websites or other commonly used forms of written or electronic media, and/or engaging a real estate or other professional to assist in renting the property, in either case, at or below market rent.

2. The property is not my secondary residence and I do not intend to use the property as a secondary residence for at least five years following the effective date of my mortgage modification. I understand that if I do use the property as a secondary residence during such five-year period, my use of the property may be considered to be inconsistent with the certifications I have made herein.

Note: The term "secondary residence" includes, without limitation, a second home, vacation home or other type of residence that I personally use or occupy on a part-time, seasonal or other basis.

3. I do not own more than five (5) single-family homes (i.e., one-to-four unit properties) (exclusive of my principal residence).

Notwithstanding the foregoing certifications, I may at any time sell the property, occupy it as my principal residence, or permit my legal dependent, parent or grandparent to occupy it as their principal residence with no rent charged or collected, none of which will be considered to be inconsistent with the certifications made herein.

This certification is effective on the earlier of the date listed below or the date the Hardship Affidavit is received by your servicer.

Initials: Borrower _____ Co-borrower _____

INFORMATION FOR GOVERNMENT MONITORING PURPOSES

The following information is requested by the federal government in order to monitor compliance with federal statutes that prohibit discrimination in housing. **You are not required to furnish this information, but are encouraged to do so. The law provides that a lender or servicer may not discriminate either on the basis of this information, or on whether you choose to furnish it.** If you furnish the information, please provide both ethnicity and race. For race, you may check more than one designation. If you do not furnish ethnicity, race, or sex, the lender or servicer is required to note the information on the basis of visual observation or surname if you have made this request for a loan modification in person. **If you do not wish to furnish the information, please check the box below.**

BORROWER	☐ I do not wish to furnish this information	CO-BORROWER	☐ I do not wish to furnish this information
Ethnicity:	☐ Hispanic or Latino ☐ Not Hispanic or Latino	*Ethnicity:*	☐ Hispanic or Latino ☐ Not Hispanic or Latino
Race:	☐ American Indian or Alaska Native ☐ Asian ☐ Black or African American ☐ Native Hawaiian or Other Pacific Islander ☐ White	*Race:*	☐ American Indian or Alaska Native ☐ Asian ☐ Black or African American ☐ Native Hawaiian or Other Pacific Islander ☐ White
Sex:	☐ Female ☐ Male	*Sex:*	☐ Female ☐ Male

To be completed by interviewer		Name/Address of Interviewer's Employer
This request was taken by: ☐ Face-to-face interview ☐ Mail ☐ Telephone ☐ Internet	*Interviewer's Name (print or type) & ID Number* *Interviewer's Signature Date* *Interviewer's Phone Number (include area code)*	

HARDSHIP AFFIDAVIT page 3	COMPLETE ALL THREE PAGES OF THIS FORM

ACKNOWLEDGEMENT AND AGREEMENT

1. That all of the information in this document is truthful and the event(s) identified on page 1 is/are the reason that I need to request a modification or forbearance of the terms of my mortgage loan, short sale or deed-in-lieu of foreclosure.

2. I understand and acknowledge that the Servicer, the U.S. Department of the Treasury, the owner or guarantor of my mortgage loan, or their respective agents may investigate the accuracy of my statements, may require me to provide additional supporting documentation and that knowingly submitting false information may violate Federal or other applicabale law.

3. I authorize and give permission to the Servicer, the U.S. Department of the Treasury, and their respective agents, to assemble and use a current consumer report on all borrowers obligated on the loan, to investigate each borrower's eligibility for MHA and the accuracy of my statements and any documentation that I provide in connection with my request for assistance. I understand that these consumer reports may include, without limitation, a credit report, and be assembled and used at any point during the application process to assess each borrower's eligibility thereafter.

4. I understand that if I have intentionally defaulted on my existing mortgage, engaged in fraud or if it is determined that any of my statements or any information contained in the documentation that I provide are materially false and that I was ineligible for assistance under MHA, the Servicer, the U.S. Department of the Treasury, or their respective agents may terminate my participation in MHA, including any right to future benefits and incentives that otherwise would have been available under the program, and also may seek other remedies available at law and in equity, such as recouping any benefits or incentives previously received.

5. I certify that any property for which I am requesting assistance is a habitable residential property that is not subject to a condemnation notice.

6. I certify that I am willing to provide all requested documents and to respond to all Servicer communications in a timely manner. I understand that time is of the essence.

7. I understand that the Servicer will use the information I provide to evaluate my eligibility for available relief options and foreclosure alternatives, but the Servicer is not obligated to offer me assistance based solely on the representations in this document or other documentation submitted in connection with my request.

8. I am willing to commit to credit counseling if it is determined that my financial hardship is related to excessive debt.

9. If I am eligible for assistance under MHA, and I accept and agree to all terms of an MHA notice, plan, or agreement, I also agree that the terms of this Acknowledgment and Agreement are incorporated into such notice, plan, or agreement by reference as if set forth therein in full. My first timely payment, if required, following my servicer's determination and notification of my eligibility or prequalification for MHA assistance will serve as my acceptance of the terms set forth in the notice, plan, or agreement sent to me.

10. I understand that my Servicer will collect and record personal information that I submit in this Hardship Affidavit and during the evaluation process, including, but not limited to, my name, address, telephone number, social security number, credit score, income, payment history, government monitoring information, and information about my account balances and activity. I understand and consent to the Servicer's disclosure of my personal information and the terms of any MHA notice, plan or agreement to the U.S. Department of the Treasury and its agents, Fannie Mae and Freddie Mac in connection with their responsibilities under MHA, companies that perform support services in conjunction with MHA, any investor, insurer, guarantor, or servicer that owns, insures, guarantees, or services my first lien or subordinate lien (if applicable) mortgage loan(s) and to any HUD-certified housing counselor.

11. I consent to being contacted concerning this request for mortgage assistance at any e-mail address or cellular or mobile telephone number I have provided to the Servicer. This includes text messages and telephone calls to my cellular or mobile telephone.

The undersigned certifies under penalty of perjury that all statements in this document are true and correct.

Borrower Signature	Social Security Number	Date of Birth	Date

Co-borrower Signature	Social Security Number	Date of Birth	Date

HOMEOWNER'S HOTLINE

If you have questions about this document or the Making Home Affordable Program, please call your servicer.

If you have questions about the program that your servicer cannot answer or need further counseling, you can call the Homeowner's HOPE™ Hotline at 1-888-995-HOPE (4673). The Hotline can help with questions about the program and offers free HUD-certified counseling services in English and Spanish.

888-995-HOPE
Homeowner's HOPE™ Hotline

NOTICE TO BORROWERS

Be advised that by signing this document you understand that any documents and information you submit to your servicer in connection with the Making Home Affordable Program are under penalty of perjury. Any misstatement of material fact made in the completion of these documents including but not limited to misstatement regarding your occupancy of your property, hardship circumstances, and/or income, expenses, or assets will subject you to potential criminal investigation and prosecution for the following crimes: perjury, false statements, mail fraud, and wire fraud. The information contained in these documents is subject to examination and verification. Any potential misrepresentation will be referred to the appropriate law enforcement authority for investigation and prosecution. By signing this document you certify, represent and agree that: "Under penalty of perjury, all documents and information I have provided to my Servicer in connection with the Making Home Affordable Program, including the documents and information regarding my eligibility for the program, are true and correct."

If you are aware of fraud, waste, abuse, mismanagement or misrepresentations affiliated with the Troubled Asset Relief Program, please contact the SIGTARP Hotline by calling 1-877-SIG-2009 (toll-free), 202-622-4559 (fax), or www.sigtarp.gov and provide them with your name, our name as your servicer, your property address, loan number and the reason for escalation. Mail can be sent to Hotline Office of the Special Inspector General for Troubled Asset Relief Program, 1801 L St. NW, Washington, DC 20220

Beware of Foreclosure Rescue Scams. Help is FREE!
-There is never a fee to get assistance or information about the Making Home Affordable Program from your lender or a HUD-approved housing counselor.
-Beware of any person or organization that asks you to pay a fee in exchange for housing counseling services or modification of a delinquent loan
-Beware of anyone who says they can "save" your home if you sign or transfer over the deed to your house. Do not sign over the deed to your property to any organization or individual unless you are working directly with your mortgage company to forgive your debt.
-Never make your mortgage payments to anyone other than your mortgage company without their approval.

Dodd–Frank Certification

HELP FOR AMERICA'S HOMEOWNERS

Dodd-Frank Certification

The following information is requested by the federal government in accordance with the Dodd-Frank Wall Street Reform and Consumer Protection Act (Pub. L. 111-203). **You are required to furnish this information.** The law provides that no person shall be eligible to begin receiving assistance from the Making Home Affordable Program, authorized under the Emergency Economic Stabilization Act of 2008 (12 U.S.C. 5201 *et seq.*), or any other mortgage assistance program authorized or funded by that Act, if such person, in connection with a mortgage or real estate transaction, has been convicted, within the last 10 years, of any one of the following: (A) felony larceny, theft, fraud, or forgery, (B) money laundering or (C) tax evasion.

I/we certify under penalty of perjury that I/we have not been convicted within the last 10 years of any one of the following in connection with a mortgage or real estate transaction:

- (a) felony larceny, theft, fraud, or forgery,
- (b) money laundering or
- (c) tax evasion.

I/we understand that the servicer, the U.S. Department of the Treasury, or their agents may investigate the accuracy of my statements by performing routine background checks, including automated searches of federal, state and county databases, to confirm that I/we have not been convicted of such crimes. I/we also understand that knowingly submitting false information may violate Federal law.

This Certificate is effective on the earlier of the date listed below or the date received by your servicer.

▸ _____   _____   _____   _____

Borrower Signature   Social Security Number   Date of Birth   Date

▸ _____   _____   _____   _____

Co-Borrower Signature   Social Security Number   Date of Birth   Date

APPENDIX

IRS Form 4506-T

New Fresno Fax Number

The fax number listed for the Internal Revenue Service RAIVS Team office in Fresno, California in Form 4506-T and Form 4506T-EZ changed from (559) 456-5876 to (559) 456-7227.

Therefore, if you filed an individual return and lived in: Alaska, Arizona, Arkansas, California, Colorado, Hawaii, Idaho, Illinois, Indiana, Iowa, Kansas, Michigan, Minnesota, Montana, Nebraska, Nevada, New Mexico, North Dakota, Oklahoma, Oregon, South Dakota, Utah, Washington, Wisconsin, or Wyoming, you must use (559) 456-7227 if you choose to request a transcript of your tax return by fax.

We encourage you to use our automated self-help service tools to quickly request transcripts. Please go to http://www.irs.gov/Individuals/Get-Transcript.

Form **4506-T**
(Rev. September 2013)
Department of the Treasury
Internal Revenue Service

Request for Transcript of Tax Return

▶ **Request may be rejected if the form is incomplete or illegible.**

OMB No. 1545-1872

Tip. Use Form 4506-T to order a transcript or other return information free of charge. See the product list below. You can quickly request transcripts by using our automated self-help service tools. Please visit us at IRS.gov and click on "Order a Return or Account Transcript" or call 1-800-908-9946. If you need a copy of your return, use **Form 4506, Request for Copy of Tax Return.** There is a fee to get a copy of your return.

1a Name shown on tax return. If a joint return, enter the name shown first.	**1b** First social security number on tax return, individual taxpayer identification number, or employer identification number (see instructions)
2a If a joint return, enter spouse's name shown on tax return.	**2b** Second social security number or individual taxpayer identification number if joint tax return

3 Current name, address (including apt., room, or suite no.), city, state, and ZIP code (see instructions)

4 Previous address shown on the last return filed if different from line 3 (see instructions)

5 If the transcript or tax information is to be mailed to a third party (such as a mortgage company), enter the third party's name, address, and telephone number.

Caution. *If the tax transcript is being mailed to a third party, ensure that you have filled in lines 6 through 9 before signing. Sign and date the form once you have filled in these lines. Completing these steps helps to protect your privacy. Once the IRS discloses your tax transcript to the third party listed on line 5, the IRS has no control over what the third party does with the information. If you would like to limit the third party's authority to disclose your transcript information, you can specify this limitation in your written agreement with the third party.*

6 **Transcript requested.** Enter the tax form number here (1040, 1065, 1120, etc.) and check the appropriate box below. Enter only one tax form number per request. ▶ _____

a **Return Transcript,** which includes most of the line items of a tax return as filed with the IRS. A tax return transcript does not reflect changes made to the account after the return is processed. Transcripts are only available for the following returns: Form 1040 series, Form 1065, Form 1120, Form 1120A, Form 1120H, Form 1120L, and Form 1120S. Return transcripts are available for the current year and returns processed during the prior 3 processing years. Most requests will be processed within 10 business days   .   .   .   .   .   . ☐

b **Account Transcript,** which contains information on the financial status of the account, such as payments made on the account, penalty assessments, and adjustments made by you or the IRS after the return was filed. Return information is limited to items such as tax liability and estimated tax payments. Account transcripts are available for most returns. Most requests will be processed within 10 business days   . ☐

c **Record of Account,** which provides the most detailed information as it is a combination of the Return Transcript and the Account Transcript. Available for current year and 3 prior tax years. Most requests will be processed within 10 business days   .   .   .   .   .   . ☐

7 **Verification of Nonfiling,** which is proof from the IRS that you **did not** file a return for the year. Current year requests are only available after June 15th. There are no availability restrictions on prior year requests. Most requests will be processed within 10 business days .   . ☐

8 **Form W-2, Form 1099 series, Form 1098 series, or Form 5498 series transcript.** The IRS can provide a transcript that includes data from these information returns. State or local information is not included with the Form W-2 information. The IRS may be able to provide this transcript information for up to 10 years. Information for the current year is generally not available until the year after it is filed with the IRS. For example, W-2 information for 2011, filed in 2012, will likely not be available from the IRS until 2013. If you need W-2 information for retirement purposes, you should contact the Social Security Administration at 1-800-772-1213. Most requests will be processed within 10 business days   . ☐

Caution. *If you need a copy of Form W-2 or Form 1099, you should first contact the payer. To get a copy of the Form W-2 or Form 1099 filed with your return, you must use Form 4506 and request a copy of your return, which includes all attachments.*

9 **Year or period requested.** Enter the ending date of the year or period, using the mm/dd/yyyy format. If you are requesting more than four years or periods, you must attach another Form 4506-T. For requests relating to quarterly tax returns, such as Form 941, you must enter each quarter or tax period separately.

_____   _____   _____   _____

Check this box if you have notified the IRS or the IRS has notified you that one of the years for which you are requesting a transcript involved **identity theft** on your federal tax return .   .   .   . ☐

Caution. Do not sign this form unless all applicable lines have been completed.

Signature of taxpayer(s). I declare that I am either the taxpayer whose name is shown on line 1a or 2a, or a person authorized to obtain the tax information requested. If the request applies to a joint return, at least one spouse must sign. If signed by a corporate officer, partner, guardian, tax matters partner, executor, receiver, administrator, trustee, or party other than the taxpayer, I certify that I have the authority to execute Form 4506-T on behalf of the taxpayer. **Note.** *For transcripts being sent to a third party, this form must be received within 120 days of the signature date.*

		Phone number of taxpayer on line 1a or 2a

Sign Here

▶ **Signature** (see instructions)   Date

▶ **Title** (if line 1a above is a corporation, partnership, estate, or trust)

▶ **Spouse's signature**   Date

For Privacy Act and Paperwork Reduction Act Notice, see page 2.   Cat. No. 37667N   Form **4506-T** (Rev. 9-2013)

Form 4506-T (Rev. 9-2013)   Page **2**

Section references are to the Internal Revenue Code unless otherwise noted.

Future Developments

For the latest information about Form 4506-T and its instructions, go to *www.irs.gov/form4506t*. Information about any recent developments affecting Form 4506-T (such as legislation enacted after we released it) will be posted on that page.

General Instructions

CAUTION. *Do not sign this form unless all applicable lines have been completed.*

Purpose of form. Use Form 4506-T to request tax return information. You can also designate (on line 5) a third party to receive the information. Taxpayers using a tax year beginning in one calendar year and ending in the following year (fiscal tax year) must file Form 4506-T to request a return transcript.

Note. If you are unsure of which type of transcript you need, request the Record of Account, as it provides the most detailed information.

Tip. Use Form 4506, Request for Copy of Tax Return, to request copies of tax returns.

Automated transcript request. You can quickly request transcripts by using our automated self-help service tools. Please visit us at IRS.gov and click on "Order a Return or Account Transcript" or call 1-800-908-9946.

Where to file. Mail or fax Form 4506-T to the address below for the state you lived in, or the state your business was in, when that return was filed. There are two address charts: one for individual transcripts (Form 1040 series and Form W-2) and one for all other transcripts.

If you are requesting more than one transcript or other product and the chart below shows two different addresses, send your request to the address based on the address of your most recent return.

Chart for individual transcripts (Form 1040 series and Form W-2 and Form 1099)

If you filed an individual return and lived in:	Mail or fax to:
Alabama, Kentucky, Louisiana, Mississippi, Tennessee, Texas, a foreign country, American Samoa, Puerto Rico, Guam, Commonwealth of the Northern Mariana Islands, the U.S. Virgin Islands, or A.P.O. or F.P.O. address	Internal Revenue Service RAIVS Team Stop 6716 AUSC Austin, TX 73301
	512-460-2272
Alaska, Arizona, Arkansas, California, Colorado, Hawaii, Idaho, Illinois, Indiana, Iowa, Kansas, Michigan, Minnesota, Montana, Nebraska, Nevada, New Mexico, North Dakota, Oklahoma, Oregon, South Dakota, Utah, Washington, Wisconsin, Wyoming	Internal Revenue Service RAIVS Team Stop 37106 Fresno, CA 93888
	559-456-5876
Connecticut, Delaware, District of Columbia, Florida, Georgia, Maine, Maryland, Massachusetts, Missouri, New Hampshire, New Jersey, New York, North Carolina, Ohio, Pennsylvania, Rhode Island, South Carolina, Vermont, Virginia, West Virginia	Internal Revenue Service RAIVS Team Stop 6705 P-6 Kansas City, MO 64999
	816-292-6102

Chart for all other transcripts

If you lived in or your business was in:	Mail or fax to:
Alabama, Alaska, Arizona, Arkansas, California, Colorado, Florida, Hawaii, Idaho, Iowa, Kansas, Louisiana, Minnesota, Mississippi, Missouri, Montana, Nebraska, Nevada, New Mexico, North Dakota, Oklahoma, Oregon, South Dakota, Texas, Utah, Washington, Wyoming, a foreign country, or A.P.O. or F.P.O. address	Internal Revenue Service RAIVS Team P.O. Box 9941 Mail Stop 6734 Ogden, UT 84409
	801-620-6922
Connecticut, Delaware, District of Columbia, Georgia, Illinois, Indiana, Kentucky, Maine, Maryland, Massachusetts, Michigan, New Hampshire, New Jersey, New York, North Carolina, Ohio, Pennsylvania, Rhode Island, South Carolina, Tennessee, Vermont, Virginia, West Virginia, Wisconsin	Internal Revenue Service RAIVS Team P.O. Box 145500 Stop 2800 F Cincinnati, OH 45250
	859-669-3592

Line 1b. Enter your employer identification number (EIN) if your request relates to a business return. Otherwise, enter the first social security number (SSN) or your individual taxpayer identification number (ITIN) shown on the return. For example, if you are requesting Form 1040 that includes Schedule C (Form 1040), enter your SSN.

Line 3. Enter your current address. If you use a P. O. box, include it on this line.

Line 4. Enter the address shown on the last return filed if different from the address entered on line 3.

Note. If the address on lines 3 and 4 are different and you have not changed your address with the IRS, file Form 8822, Change of Address. For a business address, file Form 8822-B, Change of Address or Responsible Party—Business.

Line 6. Enter only one tax form number per request.

Signature and date. Form 4506-T must be signed and dated by the taxpayer listed on line 1a or 2a. If you completed line 5 requesting the information be sent to a third party, the IRS must receive Form 4506-T within 120 days of the date signed by the taxpayer or it will be rejected. Ensure that all applicable lines are completed before signing.

Individuals. Transcripts of jointly filed tax returns may be furnished to either spouse. Only one signature is required. Sign Form 4506-T exactly as your name appeared on the original return. If you changed your name, also sign your current name.

Corporations. Generally, Form 4506-T can be signed by: (1) an officer having legal authority to bind the corporation, (2) any person designated by the board of directors or other governing body, or (3) any officer or employee on written request by any principal officer and attested to by the secretary or other officer.

Partnerships. Generally, Form 4506-T can be signed by any person who was a member of the partnership during any part of the tax period requested on line 9.

All others. See section 6103(e) if the taxpayer has died, is insolvent, is a dissolved corporation, or if a trustee, guardian, executor, receiver, or administrator is acting for the taxpayer.

Documentation. For entities other than individuals, you must attach the authorization document. For example, this could be the letter from the principal officer authorizing an employee of the corporation or the letters testamentary authorizing an individual to act for an estate.

Signature by a representative. A representative can sign Form 4506-T for a taxpayer only if the taxpayer has specifically delegated this authority to the representative on Form 2848, line 5. The representative must attach Form 2848 showing the delegation to Form 4506-T.

Privacy Act and Paperwork Reduction Act Notice. We ask for the information on this form to establish your right to gain access to the requested tax information under the Internal Revenue Code. We need this information to properly identify the tax information and respond to your request. You are not required to request any transcript; if you do request a transcript, sections 6103 and 6109 and their regulations require you to provide this information, including your SSN or EIN. If you do not provide this information, we may not be able to process your request. Providing false or fraudulent information may subject you to penalties.

Routine uses of this information include giving it to the Department of Justice for civil and criminal litigation, and cities, states, the District of Columbia, and U.S. commonwealths and possessions for use in administering their tax laws. We may also disclose this information to other countries under a tax treaty, to federal and state agencies to enforce federal nontax criminal laws, or to federal law enforcement and intelligence agencies to combat terrorism.

You are not required to provide the information requested on a form that is subject to the Paperwork Reduction Act unless the form displays a valid OMB control number. Books or records relating to a form or its instructions must be retained as long as their contents may become material in the administration of any Internal Revenue law. Generally, tax returns and return information are confidential, as required by section 6103.

The time needed to complete and file Form 4506-T will vary depending on individual circumstances. The estimated average time is: **Learning about the law or the form,** 10 min.; **Preparing the form,** 12 min.; and **Copying, assembling, and sending the form to the IRS,** 20 min.

If you have comments concerning the accuracy of these time estimates or suggestions for making Form 4506-T simpler, we would be happy to hear from you. You can write to:

Internal Revenue Service
Tax Forms and Publications Division
1111 Constitution Ave. NW, IR-6526
Washington, DC 20224

Do not send the form to this address. Instead, see *Where to file* on this page.

APPENDIX

E

IRS Form 4506T-EZ

New Fresno Fax Number

The fax number listed for the Internal Revenue Service RAIVS Team office in Fresno, California in Form 4506-T and Form 4506T-EZ changed from (559) 456-5876 to (559) 456-7227.

Therefore, if you filed an individual return and lived in: Alaska, Arizona, Arkansas, California, Colorado, Hawaii, Idaho, Illinois, Indiana, Iowa, Kansas, Michigan, Minnesota, Montana, Nebraska, Nevada, New Mexico, North Dakota, Oklahoma, Oregon, South Dakota, Utah, Washington, Wisconsin, or Wyoming, you must use (559) 456-7227 if you choose to request a transcript of your tax return by fax.

We encourage you to use our automated self-help service tools to quickly request transcripts. Please go to http://www.irs.gov/Individuals/Get-Transcript.

Form **4506T-EZ**

(Rev. January 2012)

Department of the Treasury
Internal Revenue Service

Short Form Request for Individual Tax Return Transcript

▶ **Request may not be processed if the form is incomplete or illegible.**

OMB No. 1545-2154

Tip. Use Form 4506T-EZ to order a 1040 series tax return transcript free of charge, or you can quickly request transcripts by using our automated self-help service tools. Please visit us at IRS.gov and click on "Order a Transcript" or call 1-800-908-9946.

1a Name shown on tax return. If a joint return, enter the name shown first.

1b **First social security number or individual taxpayer identification number on tax return**

2a If a joint return, enter spouse's name shown on tax return.

2b **Second social security number or individual taxpayer identification number if joint tax return**

3 Current name, address (including apt., room, or suite no.), city, state, and ZIP code (see instructions)

4 Previous address shown on the last return filed if different from line 3 (see instructions)

5 If the transcript is to be mailed to a third party (such as a mortgage company), enter the third party's name, address, and telephone number. The IRS has no control over what the third party does with the tax information.

Third party name

Telephone number

Address (including apt., room, or suite no.), city, state, and ZIP code

Caution. If the tax transcript is being mailed to a third party, ensure that you have filled in line 6 before signing. Sign and date the form once you have filled in this line. Completing this step helps to protect your privacy. Once the IRS discloses your IRS transcript to the third party listed on line 5, the IRS has no control over what the third party does with the information. If you would like to limit the third party's authority to disclose your transcript information, you can specify this limitation in your written agreement with the third party.

6 **Year(s) requested.** Enter the year(s) of the return transcript you are requesting (for example, "2008"). Most requests will be processed within 10 business days.

☐ Check this box if you have notified the IRS or the IRS has notified you that one of the years for which you are requesting a transcript involved **identity theft** on your federal tax return.

Note. *If the IRS is unable to locate a return that matches the taxpayer identity information provided above, or if IRS records indicate that the return has not been filed, the IRS may notify you or the third party that it was unable to locate a return, or that a return was not filed, whichever is applicable.*

Caution. Do not sign this form unless all applicable lines have been completed.

Signature of taxpayer(s). I declare that I am the taxpayer whose name is shown on either line 1a or 2a. If the request applies to a joint return, **either** husband or wife must sign. **Note.** *For transcripts being sent to a third party, this form must be received within 120 days of the signature date.*

Phone number of taxpayer on line 1a or 2a

Sign Here

▶ **Signature** (see instructions)   Date

▶ **Spouse's signature**   Date

For Privacy Act and Paperwork Reduction Act Notice, see page 2.   Cat. No. 54185S   Form **4506T-EZ** (Rev. 1-2012)

Section references are to the Internal Revenue Code unless otherwise noted.

What's New

The IRS has created a page on IRS.gov for information about Form 4506T-EZ at *http://www.irs.gov/form4506*. Information about any recent developments affecting Form 4506T-EZ (such as legislation enacted after we released it) will be posted on that page.

Caution. Do not sign this form unless all applicable lines have been completed.

Purpose of form. Individuals can use Form 4506T-EZ to request a tax return transcript for the current and the prior three years that includes most lines of the original tax return. The tax return transcript will not show payments, penalty assessments, or adjustments made to the originally filed return. You can also designate (on line 5) a third party (such as a mortgage company) to receive a transcript. Form 4506T-EZ cannot be used by taxpayers who file Form 1040 based on a tax year beginning in one calendar year and ending in the following year (fiscal tax year). Taxpayers using a fiscal tax year must file Form 4506-T, Request for Transcript of Tax Return, to request a return transcript.

Use Form 4506-T to request tax return transcripts, tax account information, W-2 information, 1099 information, verification of non-filing, and record of account.

Automated transcript request. You can quickly request transcripts by using our automated self-help service tools. Please visit us at IRS.gov and click on "Order a Transcript" or call 1-800-908-9946.

Where to file. Mail or fax Form 4506T-EZ to the address below for the state you lived in when the return was filed.

If you are requesting more than one transcript or other product and the chart below shows two different addresses, send your request to the address based on the address of your most recent return.

If you filed an individual return and lived in:	Mail or fax to the "Internal Revenue Service" at:
Alabama, Kentucky, Louisiana, Mississippi, Tennessee, Texas, a foreign country, American Samoa, Puerto Rico, Guam, the Commonwealth of the Northern Mariana Islands, the U.S. Virgin Islands, or A.P.O. or F.P.O. address	RAIVS Team Stop 6716 AUSC Austin, TX 73301 512-460-2272
Alaska, Arizona, Arkansas, California, Colorado, Hawaii, Idaho, Illinois, Indiana, Iowa, Kansas, Michigan, Minnesota, Montana, Nebraska, Nevada, New Mexico, North Dakota, Oklahoma, Oregon, South Dakota, Utah, Washington, Wisconsin, Wyoming	RAIVS Team Stop 37106 Fresno, CA 93888 559-456-5876
Connecticut, Delaware, District of Columbia, Florida, Georgia, Maine, Maryland, Massachusetts, Missouri, New Hampshire, New Jersey, New York, North Carolina, Ohio, Pennsylvania, Rhode Island, South Carolina, Vermont, Virginia, West Virginia	RAIVS Team Stop 6705 P-6 Kansas City, MO 64999 816-292-6102

Line 1b. Enter your employer identification number (EIN) if your request relates to a business return. Otherwise, enter the first social security number (SSN) or your individual taxpayer identification number (ITIN) shown on the return. For example, if you are requesting Form 1040 that includes Schedule C (Form 1040), enter your SSN.

Line 3. Enter your current address. If you use a P.O. box, include it on this line.

Line 4. Enter the address shown on the last return filed if different from the address entered on line 3.

Note. If the address on lines 3 and 4 are different and you have not changed your address with the IRS, file Form 8822, Change of Address.

Signature and date. Form 4506T-EZ must be signed and dated by the taxpayer listed on line 1a or 2a. If you completed line 5 requesting the information be sent to a third party, the IRS must receive Form 4506T-EZ within 120 days of the date signed by the taxpayer or it will be rejected. Ensure that all applicable lines are completed before signing.

Transcripts of jointly filed tax returns may be furnished to either spouse. Only one signature is required. Sign Form 4506T-EZ exactly as your name appeared on the original return. If you changed your name, also sign your current name.

Privacy Act and Paperwork Reduction Act Notice. We ask for the information on this form to establish your right to gain access to the requested tax information under the Internal Revenue Code. We need this information to properly identify the tax information and respond to your request. If you request a transcript, sections 6103 and 6109 require you to provide this information, including your SSN. If you do not provide this information, we may not be able to process your request. Providing false or fraudulent information may subject you to penalties.

Routine uses of this information include giving it to the Department of Justice for civil and criminal litigation, and cities, states, the District of Columbia, and U.S. commonwealths and possessions for use in administering their tax laws. We may also disclose this information to other countries under a tax treaty, to federal and state agencies to enforce federal nontax criminal laws, or to federal law enforcement and intelligence agencies to combat terrorism.

You are not required to provide the information requested on a form that is subject to the Paperwork Reduction Act unless the form displays a valid OMB control number. Books or records relating to a form or its instructions must be retained as long as their contents may become material in the administration of any Internal Revenue law. Generally, tax returns and return information are confidential, as required by section 6103.

The time needed to complete and file Form 4506T-EZ will vary depending on individual circumstances. The estimated average time is: **Learning about the law or the form,** 9 min.; **Preparing the form,** 18 min.; and **Copying, assembling, and sending the form to the IRS,** 20 min.

If you have comments concerning the accuracy of these time estimates or suggestions for making Form 4506T-EZ simpler, we would be happy to hear from you. You can write to:

Internal Revenue Service
Tax Products Coordinating Committee
SE:W:CAR:MP:T:M:S
1111 Constitution Ave. NW, IR-6526
Washington, DC 20224

Do not send the form to this address. Instead, see *Where to file* on this page.

APPENDIX

F

Short Sale Notice

HELP FOR AMERICA'S HOMEOWNERS.

MAKING HOME AFFORDABLE

[Name of Servicer]
[Address of Servicer]

[Loan #]
[Servicer FAX]
[Servicer Email]

[Date]

[Name of Borrower]
[Name of Co-Borrower]
[Address of Borrower]

[Borrower Phone]
[Borrower Email]

Dear [borrower and co-borrower name(s)]:

If you are looking for help selling your residential property and avoiding foreclosure, the federal government has introduced the **Home Affordable Foreclosure Alternatives** (HAFA) Program to help you. As your mortgage servicer, we are offering you the opportunity to participate in this program by utilizing HAFA's short sale option.

Home Affordable Foreclosure Alternatives Program – Short Sale
A "short sale" is specifically designed to help borrowers who are unable to afford their first mortgage and want to sell their residential property to avoid foreclosure, even if the sale price may not pay off the amount owed on their mortgage. A short sale requires a number of parties (you, the buyer, your real estate broker, and sometimes mortgage insurance companies and other lenders) to work together to make this option successful. However, it could be a good solution for your current situation.

How Does a Short Sale Work?
- **Pre-Sale**—We will start by approving a list price for your property or give you the acceptable sale proceeds (the minimum amount that we must receive after sales costs) from the sale of the property. We will also identify the sales costs (broker commissions and closing costs) that may be deducted from the final sales price. You then list your property (like any home sale) with a local real estate broker at the approved price.
- **Offer**—When you get an offer on your property, you will submit the required documentation and we will approve the sale if it is in line with what we agreed to.
- **Closing**—Once the sale closes, we will release you from all responsibilities for repaying your mortgage. Plus, if your property is occupied as a principal residence by (i) you or (ii) a tenant (or legal dependent, parent or grandparent who is living in the property rent free) ("Tenant") who will be required to vacate the property as a condition of the sale, you or your Tenant may receive $3,000 to help pay moving expenses. (The check will be paid to the occupant by the settlement agent as part of the closing.) In the event there is any money left over from the sale after paying the entire amount you owe on the mortgage plus the approved sale costs, you or your Tenant will not be eligible to receive the $3,000 relocation assistance.

To Participate in the Short Sale Program
Please note, there is no guarantee that your property will sell under this program, and you are responsible for determining whether you want to sell your property for the price and terms described in this letter. The following pages detail your responsibilities, additional information on the short sale process and the Terms and Conditions. **Additionally, this letter constitutes an agreement between us and you ("Agreement") so please read it carefully and completely.**

If you agree to the terms of the Agreement and want to proceed with a short sale, you must complete, sign and return the Agreement back to us. If you have questions, please contact us directly between the hours of [insert hours] at [insert toll free number.]

Sincerely,
[Servicer Name]

Important Program Information 　MAKING HOME AFFORDABLE

Short Sale Program—Your Responsibilities

> **To Accept This Offer**
>
> - Please sign and return this Agreement. All owners of the property must sign this Agreement.
> - Obtain your broker's signature to acknowledge this Agreement, because your broker plays an important role selling your property. The Short Sale Program sections (pages 2-4) contain important information that you and your broker will need to review and discuss.
> - Include a copy of your signed listing agreement.
> - Include information on other liens secured by the property (such as home equity loans, homeowner association liens, tax liens or judgments).
> - [*Insert only if applicable:*] Complete and sign the Hardship Affidavit form.

You have until [*insert date 120 calendar days from the date of this letter*] to sell your property. After that date, this Agreement terminates, unless it is extended by us. During this time you have certain responsibilities. You must:

❶ Keep your property in good condition and repair and cooperate with your broker to show it to potential buyers. If your property is occupied by a Tenant, the Tenant must also satisfy this requirement.

❷ [*Insert only if applicable:*] Make partial mortgage payments of $_____ by the first day of each month beginning on _____ 1, 20___ until your property is sold and title is transferred. While you are selling your property, you still legally owe the full amount of your current monthly mortgage payment. However, as part of this Agreement, we will accept this reduced payment until the house is sold and closes or this Agreement expires. These payments do not constitute a modification of your mortgage.

❸ Be able to provide the buyer of your property with clear title. To start, determine if you have other loans, judgments or liens secured by your property, such as a home-equity line of credit or a second mortgage. If there are such liens, you will need to either pay these loans off in full or negotiate with the lien holders to release them before the closing date. Under this program, you must make sure other lien holders will agree not to pursue other legal action related to the pay off of their lien, such as a deficiency judgment. You can get help from your broker to negotiate with the other lien holders.

❹ We may allow an aggregate of up to [*insert the lesser of $8,500 or maximum amount allowable by investor*] to be paid from the sale proceeds to help get subordinate mortgage lien releases and an aggregate of up to [*choose one as applicable*] [$_____] OR [_____% of gross sales proceeds] [*insert amount or percentage, as applicable and as determined by servicer*] to be paid from sale proceeds to help get subordinate non-mortgage lien releases. If you have these types of liens or loans on your property, please gather any paperwork you have (such as your last statement) and send it to us when you return this signed Agreement. Remember, clearing these other liens and delivering clear and marketable title is your responsibility.

❺ At several stages of the short sale process, such as after an offer is received, you will need to complete some paperwork. You are responsible for returning all documents within the time allowed in this Agreement.

If you fulfill these responsibilities, we will postpone any foreclosure sale during the period of this Agreement.

Short Sale Program—Additional Information

- You can't list the property with or sell it to anyone that you are related to or have a close personal or business relationship with. In legal language, it must be an "arm's length transaction." If you have a real estate license you can't earn a commission by listing your own property. You may not have any agreements to receive a portion of the commission or the sales price after closing. Any buyer of your property must agree to not sell the property within 90 calendar days of the date it is sold by you. You may not have any expectation that you will be able to buy or rent [*servicer may delete "or rent" in accordance with investor guidelines*] your property back after the closing. Any knowing violation of the arm's length transaction prohibition may be a violation of federal law.

- We will need to talk to your broker and others involved in the sale. By signing this Agreement, you are authorizing us to communicate and share personal financial information about your mortgage, credit history, subordinate liens, and plans for relocation with your broker and other third parties that could be involved in the transaction including employees of the United States Department of the Treasury and its financial agents, Fannie Mae and Freddie Mac.

- The difference between the remaining amount of principal you owe and the amount that we receive from the sale must be reported to the Internal Revenue Service (IRS) on Form 1099C, as debt forgiveness. In some cases, debt forgiveness could be taxed as income. The amount, if any, we pay you or your tenant for moving expenses may also be reported as income. We suggest that you contact the IRS or your tax preparer to determine if you may have any tax liability.

- We will follow standard industry practice and report to the major credit reporting agencies that your mortgage was settled for less than the full payment. We have no control over, or responsibility for the impact of this report on your credit score. To learn more about the potential impact of a short sale on your credit you may want to go to http://www.ftc.gov/bcp/edu/pubs/consumer/credit/cre24.shtm.

[*Insert optional Deed-in-Lieu language if applicable:*

If by the termination date of this Agreement, you have complied with all your responsibilities but are unable to sell your property, we will allow you to convey ownership of all of the real property securing your mortgage loan to us to satisfy the total amount due on your first mortgage. While this action, called a deed-in-lieu of foreclosure, will not allow you to keep your property, it will prevent you from going through a foreclosure sale and it will release you from all responsibility to repay the mortgage debt. Additionally, provided the other terms of this Agreement are complied with, you or your Tenant may still be eligible to receive $3,000 to help with moving expenses.

All occupants must vacate the property unless the sales contract provides otherwise. In addition, you must provide clear and marketable title with a general warranty deed or local equivalent by [[*insert date at least 30 days after the date of this Agreement if a deed-for-lease is not applicable*] or [*insert date that the applicable deed-for-lease terminates if applicable*]]. You must leave the house in broom clean condition, free of interior and exterior trash, debris or damage, and all personal belongings must be removed from the property. The yard must be clean and neat and you must deliver all the keys and controls, such as garage door openers, to us. You may be required to sign standard pre-closing documents as well as attend a closing of the conveyance of your property where all borrowers on the mortgage must be present.

You must also be able to deliver marketable title free of any other liens. We will allow (i) up to [*insert the lesser of $8,500 or maximum amount allowable by investor*] in aggregate for all subordinate mortgage liens and (ii) up to [*choose one as applicable*] [$_____] OR [____% of gross sales proceeds] [*insert amount or percentage as applicable and as determined by servicer*] in aggregate for all subordinate non-mortgage liens, in each case to be deducted from sales proceeds to pay, in order of priority, such subordinate lien holders to release their liens. We require each subordinate lien holder to release you from personal liability for the loans in order for the sale to qualify for this program, but we do not take any responsibility for ensuring that the lien holders do not seek to enforce

personal liability against you. Therefore, we recommend that you take steps to satisfy yourself that the subordinate lien holders release you from personal liability.

By signing this letter, you are agreeing not only to a short sale but also to a deed-in-lieu of foreclosure if a short sale is not successful. If you have any questions about the deed-in-lieu of foreclosure, please call us before signing and returning this letter.]

Short Sale Program—Receiving/Accepting an Offer

When you receive an offer on your property, within the next 3 business days, you will send us a Request to Approve a Short Sale (RASS) form, a copy of which is attached to this Agreement as Exhibit A1. You will also need to send along a copy of the signed purchase offer and evidence that the buyer has funds to purchase the property, such as a letter that the buyer is approved for a mortgage loan.

Additionally, if you or a Tenant occupy the property as a principal residence and you wish to receive (or have your Tenant receive) relocation assistance, you must provide evidence of occupancy and the other documentation described below in Program Terms and Conditions.
Within 10 business days of our receipt of these documents, we will approve the sale if it is within the terms and conditions of this Agreement and any other liens are released.

When the sale closes in accordance with this Agreement, we will accept the net sale proceeds (all the funds that remain after the approved sales costs have been paid) in full satisfaction of your mortgage with us and will release you from all future liability.

We hope you decide to take advantage of this short sale option. If you or your broker have any questions about this Agreement please call us at [insert servicer phone number].

If you would like to speak with a counselor about this program, call the Homeowner's HOPE™ Hotline 1-888-995-HOPE (4673). The Homeowner's HOPE™ Hotline offers free HUD-certified counseling services and is available 24/7 in English and Spanish. Other languages are available by appointment.

Short Sale Agreement Terms and Conditions

1. **List Price or Acceptable Sale Proceeds.** [*Choose one and delete unnecessary text.*] [You agree to list the property in "as is" condition for [dollar amount].] OR [We will accept a sales contract where the proceeds from the sale, less the expenses stated in paragraph 5. *Allowable Costs*, nets [dollar amount].] We are not responsible for the accuracy of the list price and have no responsibility to you in the event the property is not sold. We may require you to adjust the list price or other offer terms.

2. **Listing Agreement.** The listing agreement must include the following clauses:
    a. **Cancellation Clause.** "Seller may cancel this Agreement prior to the ending date of the listing period without advance notice to the broker, and without payment of a commission or any other consideration, if the property is conveyed to the mortgage insurer or the mortgage holder."
    b. **Listing Agreement Contingency Clause**. "Sale of the property is contingent on written agreement to all sale terms by the mortgage holder and the mortgage insurer (if applicable)."

3. **Property Maintenance and Expenses.** You are responsible for all property maintenance and expenses during the listing period including utilities, assessments, association dues and costs for interior and exterior upkeep required to show the property to its best advantage. Additionally, until ownership is transferred, you must report any and all property damage to us and file a hazard insurance claim for covered damage. Unless insurance proceeds are used to pay for repairs or personal property losses as provided in the mortgage documents, we may require that they be applied to reduce the mortgage debt.

4. [*Insert only if applicable:*] **Partial Mortgage Payments.** Beginning on _____ 1, 20___, you will be required to make partial mortgage payments of $_____ by the first day of each month during the term of the Agreement and pending transfer of property ownership. You are legally obligated to make the full amount of your current monthly mortgage payments. However, we will accept this reduced partial payment until the house is sold or this Agreement expires. The partial mortgage payments do not constitute a modification of your mortgage.

5. **Allowable Costs that May be Deducted from Gross Sale Proceeds**
    a. **Closing Costs.** The closing costs paid by you or on your behalf as seller must be reasonable and customary for the market. [*Choose one and delete unnecessary text.*] [Acceptable closing costs, including the commission, which may be deducted from the gross sale proceeds may not exceed $_____.] OR [Acceptable closing costs, including the commission, which may be deducted from the gross sale proceeds may not exceed ____% of the list price.] OR [Closing costs which may be deducted from the gross sale proceeds are limited to title search and escrow expenses usually paid by the seller; reasonable settlement escrow/attorney's fees; transfer taxes and recording fees usually paid by the seller; termite inspection and treatment as required by law or custom; pro-rated real property taxes; and, real estate commissions of ____ percent of the contract sales price [add other closing costs that may be included].]
    b. **Subordinate Liens.** We will allow up to an aggregate of [*insert the lesser of $8,500 or maximum amount allowable by investor*], for subordinate mortgage lien holders, and up to an aggregate of [*choose one as applicable*] [$_____] OR [_____% of gross sales proceeds] [*insert amount or percentage as applicable and as determined by servicer*] for subordinate non-mortgage lien holders, in each case, to be deducted from the gross sale proceeds to pay such subordinate lien holders to release their liens. We require each subordinate lien holder to release you from personal liability for the loans in order for the sale to qualify for this program, but we do not take any responsibility for ensuring that the lien holders do not seek to enforce personal liability against you. Therefore, we recommend that you take steps to satisfy yourself that the subordinate lien holders release you from personal liability.
    c. **Real Estate Commissions.** We will allow to be paid from sale proceeds, real estate commissions of _____ percent [*note - not to exceed 6%*] of the contract sales price, to be paid to the listing and selling brokers involved in the transaction. Neither you nor the buyer may receive a commission. Any commission that would otherwise be paid to you or the buyer must be reduced from the commission due on sale. [*Insert if applicable:* Please note: We have retained a vendor to assist your listing broker with the sale. The vendor and your listing broker will work together on your behalf to facilitate the sale process. Vendor fees or charges will not be charged to you and will not be deducted from the real estate commission. Additionally, any outsourcing firm or third party retained as an agent for us may not charge (either

Program Terms And Conditions
MAKING HOME AFFORDABLE

directly or indirectly) any outsourcing fee, short sale negotiation fee, or similar fee in connection with the short sale.]

  d. **Occupant Relocation Assistance.** Please check one box and initial below:
- ☐ You are not requesting relocation assistance.
- ☐ You are requesting relocation assistance and you certify, under penalty of perjury, that the property is occupied as a principal residence by (i) you or (ii) a tenant or (iii) your legal dependent, parent or grandparent who is living in the property rent-free .

    Initials: **Borrower** _____ **Co-borrower** _____

6. To be eligible for relocation assistance, the occupant must be required to vacate as a condition of the sale. In addition, you must provide (i) evidence that the property is your/their principal residence, which in the case of a Tenant may include information concerning the tenant, a copy of the lease agreement or other evidence of occupancy; and (ii) a certification signed by each occupant that will receive relocation assistance, attesting to the occupant's compliance with Section 1481 of the Dodd-Frank Wall Street Reform and Consumer Protection Act (Pub.L. 111-203) (the Dodd-Frank Certification). Upon request we will provide you with a Dodd-Frank Certification form(s). If you fail to deliver the Dodd-Frank Certification at least ___ days prior to the closing of the sale of the property, the incentive payment will not be paid. Upon your compliance with the terms of this Agreement, we will instruct the settlement agent to pay the occupant from the sale proceeds at the same time that all other payments, including the payoff of our first mortgage, are disbursed by the settlement agent. Only one payment per household is provided for the relocation assistance, regardless of the number of occupants.

7. **Sales Contracts.** Within three business days of a bona-fide purchase offer, you must submit a Request for Approval of a Short Sale, which is attached as Exhibit A1, along with a copy of a fully executed Sales Contract, all addenda and Buyer's documentation of funds or Buyer's pre-approval or commitment letter on letterhead from a lender.

8. **Parties to the Sale**. The Sales Contract must contain the following clauses: "Seller and Buyer each represent that the sale is an "arm's length" transaction and the Seller and Buyer are unrelated to each other by family, marriage or commercial enterprise." "The Buyer agrees not to sell the property within 90 days of closing of this sale."

9. **Closing.** The closing must occur within ____ calendar days of the Sales Contract execution date.

10. **Foreclosure Sale Suspension**. We may initiate or continue the foreclosure process as permitted by the mortgage documents; however, we will suspend any foreclosure sale date until the expiration date of this Agreement or the date of closing of an approved short sale, whichever is later, provided you continue to abide by the terms and conditions of this Agreement.

11. **Satisfaction and Release of Liability.** If all of the terms and conditions of this Agreement are met, upon sale and settlement of the property, servicer will prepare and send for recording a lien release in full satisfaction of the mortgage, foregoing all rights to personal liability or deficiency judgment.

12. [*Insert only if applicable.*] **Mortgage Insurer or Guarantor Approval.** The terms and conditions of the sale are subject to the written approval of the mortgage insurer or guarantor.

13. **Termination of this Agreement.** Unless otherwise agreed by the parties, this Agreement will terminate on [*insert date*]. We may also terminate this Agreement at any time if:
  a. Your financial situation improves significantly, you qualify for loan modification, you bring the account current or you pay off the mortgage in full.
  b. You or your broker fails to act in good faith in marketing and /or closing on the sale of the property, or otherwise fails to abide by the terms of this Agreement.
  c. A significant change occurs to the property's condition or value.
  d. There is evidence of fraud or misrepresentation.
  e. You file for bankruptcy and the Bankruptcy Court declines to approve the Agreement.
  f. Litigation is initiated or threatened that could affect title to the property or interfere with a valid conveyance.
  g. You or your tenant, if applicable, fail to cooperate with the listing broker or make the property available for marketing.

h.   [*Insert only if applicable:*] You do not make the payments required under this Agreement.

14. **Settlement of a Debt**. The proposed transaction represents our attempt to reach a settlement of the delinquent mortgage. You are choosing to enter into this Agreement even though there is no guarantee that the transaction will be successful. In the event this transaction is unsuccessful, we may exercise our remedies under the mortgage, including foreclosure.

Program Agreement

MAKING HOME AFFORDABLE

Short Sale Agreement

By signing this Agreement, you are agreeing to a short sale. If you have any questions about the short sale, please call us before signing and returning this Agreement.

PLEASE READ THIS AGREEMENT CAREFULLY BEFORE YOU SIGN, BECAUSE IT AFFECTS YOUR LEGAL RIGHTS.

Borrower Acknowledgement of Risks, Conditions and Contingencies. In signing and returning this Short Sale Agreement, I/we agree to all the stated terms and conditions.

Borrower Signature	Date	Co- Borrower Signature	Date

Printed Name	Printed Name

Acknowledgement by Listing Broker

The undersigned listing broker ("Broker") is not a party of the Short Sale Agreement ("Agreement") above, but acknowledges that the Broker:

1. Has been retained by the borrower for the sale of the property.
2. Has reviewed the terms and conditions of the Agreement above.
3. Agrees that in the event of a conflict between the terms of the listing agreement and the terms agreed to by the borrower in the Agreement above, the listing agreement will be deemed amended to conform to the terms of the Agreement.
4. Acknowledges that pursuant to the Agreement, the Servicer will not review a sales contract unless a Request for Approval of Short Sale, attached as Exhibit A1, is completed.

Listing Broker Name	Listing Broker Signature
Address:	License #:
	Office Phone:
	Cell Phone:
Date:	E-mail Address:

If you have questions, please contact us directly between the hours of [insert hours] at [insert toll free number].

Signature of Servicer Representative	Title

Printed Name of Servicer Representative	Date

If you would like to speak with a counselor about this program, call the Homeowner's HOPE™ Hotline 1-888-995-HOPE (4673). The Homeowner's HOPE™ Hotline offers free HUD-certified counseling services and is available 24/7 in English and Spanish. Other languages are available by appointment.

NOTICE TO BORROWER

Be advised that by signing this document you understand that any documents and information you submit to your servicer in connection with the Making Home Affordable Program are under penalty of perjury. Any misstatement of material fact made in the completion of these documents including but not limited to misstatement regarding your occupancy in your home, hardship circumstances, and/or income, expenses, or assets will subject you to potential criminal investigation and prosecution for the following crimes: perjury, false statements, mail fraud, and wire fraud. The information contained in these documents is subject to examination and verification. Any potential misrepresentation will be referred to the appropriate law enforcement authority for investigation and prosecution. By signing this document you certify, represent and agree that:" Under penalty of perjury, all documents and information I have provided to Lender in connection with the Making Home Affordable Program, including the documents and information regarding my eligibility for the program, are true and correct."

If you are aware of fraud, waste, abuse, mismanagement or misrepresentations affiliated with the Troubled Asset Relief Program, please contact the SIGTARP Hotline by calling 1-877-SIG-2009 (toll-free), 202-622-4559 (fax), or www.sigtarp.gov. Mail can be sent Hotline Office of the Special Inspector General for Troubled Asset Relief Program, 1801 L St. NW, Washington, DC 20220.

APPENDIX

G

Acknowledgment of Request for Short Sale

HELP FOR AMERICA'S HOMEOWNERS.

MAKING HOME AFFORDABLE

[Name of Servicer]   [Name of Borrower]
[Address of Servicer]   [Name of Co-Borrower]
                                                      [Address of Borrower]

[Loan #]
[Servicer FAX]   [Borrower Phone]
[Servicer Email]   [Borrower Email]

[Date]

RE: Acknowledgement of Request for Short Sale

You have provided us with a copy of an executed sales contract (the "Contract") for the short sale of your residential property and requested that you be considered for participation in the federal government's **Home Affordable Foreclosure Alternatives** ("HAFA") Program. This notice ("Notice") acknowledges our receipt of the Contract and provides you important information regarding the terms and conditions with which a HAFA short sale must comply if we approve the Contract. **This Notice merely acknowledges receipt of your Contract and is not an approval of the Contract.** We anticipate responding to your request for approval within 30 days of *[insert as applicable:* [of your request] *[or]* [of receipt of the Hardship Affidavit described below]. This Notice describes the terms that will be applicable only in the event we approve the Contract.

[*Insert the following if the borrower has not delivered a Hardship Affidavit and the borrower has a Pre-determined Hardship:*] Please complete, sign and return the attached Hardship Affidavit form with the other documents you provide at closing. This form is your official certification of the financial hardship you have experienced.

[*Insert the following if the borrower has not delivered a Hardship Affidavit and the borrower does not have a Pre-determined Hardship:*] Please complete, sign and return the attached Hardship Affidavit form to us at the address on the next page within 14 calendar days. This form is your official certification of the financial hardship you have experienced. We will only begin considering your request for approval of the Contract upon receipt of the completed and signed Hardship Affidavit.

[*If applicable:*] Please [also] provide [names of missing documents] to us at the address below within 14 calendar days. If we do not receive these documents, we cannot proceed with the evaluation.

If you have not previously contacted us regarding eligibility for a loan modification, you should consider this alternative. Under the Home Affordable Modification Program ("HAMP"), you may qualify for a modification with affordable and sustainable monthly payments that would allow you to keep your property. Please contact us by [*insert date 14 calendar days from date of this Notice*] if you wish to be considered for a loan modification.

If you have questions, please contact us directly between the hours of [insert hours] at [insert toll free number.]

Sincerely,

[Servicer Name]

Important Program Information

The borrower and co-borrower, if applicable ("you"), of the above loan contacted the Servicer ("we") because your mortgage payments are no longer affordable and you would like to avoid foreclosure. After listing your residential property for sale, you executed the Contract and have now requested that we approve it. However, the proceeds from the sale may not be sufficient to pay off your loan. This Notice describes the requirements a short sale must meet in order to participate in the HAFA Short Sale Program. **This Notice does not constitute an approval of the Contract**. If we ultimately approve the Contract and you comply with the terms described below, we will accept the net sale proceeds from the sale of your property as the payoff of the mortgage loan even though the proceeds are expected to be less than the full amount due. Please submit all required documents to us at the following address: [insert servicer address].

Short Sale Program – If a Contract is Approved the Following Terms and Conditions will Apply:

1.   **Allowable Costs that May be Deducted from Gross Sale Proceeds**

   a.   **Closing Costs.** The closing costs paid by you or on your behalf as seller must be reasonable and customary for the market. [*Choose one and delete unnecessary text*.] [Acceptable closing costs, including the commission, which may be deducted from the gross sale proceeds may not exceed $_____.] OR [Acceptable closing costs, including the commission, which may be deducted from the gross sale proceeds may not exceed ____% of the list price.] OR [Closing costs which may be deducted from the gross sale proceeds are limited to title search and escrow expenses usually paid by the seller; reasonable settlement escrow/attorney's fees; transfer taxes and recording fees usually paid by the seller; termite inspection and treatment as required by law or custom; pro-rated real property taxes; and, negotiated real estate commissions of ____ percent [*note – not to exceed 6%*] of the contract sales price [add other closing costs that may be included].]

   b.   **Subordinate Liens.** We have the option of allowing a total of up to [*insert the lesser of $8,500 or maximum amount allowable by investor*] to be paid from the sale proceeds to help get subordinate mortgage lien releases and a total of up to [*choose one as applicable*] [$_____] OR [_____% of gross sales proceeds] [*insert amount or percentage, as applicable and as determined by servicer*] to be paid from sale proceeds to help get subordinate non-mortgage lien releases. As described above, if you have these types of liens or loans on your property, please gather any paperwork you have (such as your last statement) and send it to us promptly. Remember, clearing these other liens and delivering clear and marketable title is your responsibility. We require each subordinate lien holder to release you from personal liability for the loans in order for the sale to qualify for this program, but we do not take any responsibility for ensuring that the lien holders do not seek to enforce personal liability against you. Therefore, we recommend that you take steps to satisfy yourself that the subordinate lien holders release you from personal liability.

   c.   **Real Estate Commissions.** We will allow to be paid from sale proceeds, real estate commissions as stated in the listing agreement between you and your broker, not to exceed six percent (6%) of the contract sales price, to be paid to the listing and selling brokers involved in the transaction. Neither you nor the buyer may receive a commission. Any commission that would otherwise be paid to you or the buyer must be reduced from the commission due on sale. [*Insert if applicable*: Please note: We have retained a vendor to assist your listing broker with the sale. The vendor and your listing broker will work together on your behalf to facilitate the sale process. Vendor fees or charges will not be charged to you and will not be deducted from the real estate commission. Additionally, any outsourcing firm or third party retained as an agent for us may not charge (either directly or indirectly) any outsourcing fee, short sale negotiation fee, or similar fee in connection with the short sale.]

   d.   [*Section to be omitted if the property is vacant*]: **Occupant Relocation Assistance**. If you or a Tenant occupy the property as a principal residence and you wish to receive (or have your Tenant receive) relocation assistance, you must inform us in writing of your request. Please send us an e-mail indicating that you will request relocation assistance to the following address [insert e-mail address of servicer's SPOC for this borrower]. Alternatively, you may send a signed, hard copy of your request to the mailing address listed above. You will be required to certify under penalty of perjury at closing that the property

is occupied as a principal residence by (i) yourself; (ii) a Tenant; or (iii) your legal dependent, parent or grandparent who is living in the property rent-free.

To receive relocation assistance, the occupant must be required to vacate as a condition of the sale. In addition, you must provide (i) evidence that the property is your/their principal residence, which in the case of a Tenant may include information concerning the tenant, a copy of the lease agreement or other evidence of occupancy; and (ii) a certification signed by each occupant that will receive relocation assistance attesting to the occupant's compliance with Section 1481 of the Dodd-Frank Wall Street Reform and Consumer Protection Act (Pub. L. 111-203) (the Dodd-Frank Certification). We will provide you with a Dodd-Frank Certification form(s). If you fail to deliver the Dodd-Frank Certification at least ___ days prior to the closing of the sale of the property, the relocation assistance will not be paid. Upon your compliance with the conditions of the sale, we will instruct the settlement agent to pay the occupant from the sale proceeds at the same time that all other payments, including the payoff of our first mortgage, are disbursed by the settlement agent. Only one payment per household is provided for the relocation assistance, regardless of the number of occupants.

2. **Property Maintenance and Expenses.** You are responsible for all property maintenance and expenses of your property until the closing of an approved short sale, including utilities, assessments, association dues, and costs for interior and exterior maintenance. Additionally, you must report any and all property damage to us and file a hazard insurance claim for covered damage. Unless insurance proceeds are used to pay for repairs or personal property losses, we may require that they be applied to reduce the mortgage debt.

3. **Short Sale Affidavit**. At closing the buyer and seller will be required to execute an affidavit certifying that the sale is an "arm's length" transaction and the seller and buyer are unrelated to each other by family, marriage or commercial enterprise. The affidavit will also include an agreement by the buyer not to sell the property within 30 days of closing of the sale, or between 31 and 90 calendar days of the sale for a price greater than 120 percent of the gross sales price and an affidavit of occupancy.

4. **Foreclosure Sale Suspension**. We will postpone any foreclosure sale until a decision is made plus any extensions that we may grant in writing, or until the closing date of an approved short sale, whichever is later. Please note that we may still initiate foreclosure or continue with existing foreclosure proceedings as permitted by the mortgage documents during this period.

5. **Satisfaction and Release of Liability.** If all of the terms and conditions of the approved short sale are met, upon sale and settlement of the property, we will prepare and send to the settlement agent for recording a lien release in full satisfaction of the mortgage, foregoing all rights to pursue a deficiency judgment.

6. [*Insert for borrowers that have not provided a Hardship Affidavit and who have a predetermined hardship:*] **Consent to Discuss Your Records**. We will need to talk to your broker and others involved in the sale. To authorize us to communicate and share your personal financial information about your mortgage, credit history, subordinate liens, and plans for relocation with your broker and other third parties that could be involved in the transaction, please [*provide instructions for delivery of authorization language. The text immediately below can be used as a model for the authorization requested from the borrower*]. It is necessary for us to receive this consent in order to proceed with the short sale.

   "I, [name], hereby authorize [insert servicer name] to communicate and share my personal financial information about my mortgage, credit history, subordinate liens, and plans for relocation with my broker and other third parties who may be involved in my proposed short sale and related transactions, including, but not limited to, employees of the United States Department of the Treasury and its financial agents, Fannie Mae and Freddie Mac."]

7. [*Insert only if applicable:*] **Mortgage Insurer or Guarantor Approval.** The terms and conditions of the short sale are subject to the written approval of the mortgage insurer or guarantor.

Important Program Information  MAKING HOME AFFORDABLE

8. [*Insert only if applicable:*] **Partial Mortgage Payments**. You must make partial mortgage payments of $_____ by the first day of each month beginning on _____ 1, 20___ until the sale of your property closes and title is transferred. Until title is transferred, you still legally owe the full amount of your current monthly mortgage payment. However, as part of the short sale process, we will accept this reduced payment until title transfer. These payments do not constitute a modification of your mortgage.

9. **Termination of Short Sale.** Unless otherwise stipulated by us in writing, any approval of the short sale may be terminated if:

    a. You fail to authorize us to discuss your personal financial information with your broker or others involved in the sale;

    b. Your financial situation improves significantly, you qualify for a modification, you bring the account current or you pay off the mortgage in full;

    c. You or your broker fails to act in good faith in closing on the sale of the property or otherwise fails to abide by the terms of this letter;

    d. A significant change occurs to the property's condition or value;

    e. There is evidence of fraud or misrepresentation;

    f. You file for bankruptcy and the Bankruptcy Court declines to approve the short sale transaction;

    g. Litigation is initiated or threatened that could affect title to the property or interfere with a valid conveyance; or

    h. [*Insert only if applicable:*] You do not make the payments required as a condition of the short sale.

    i. [*Insert only if applicable:*] You do not sign and return the attached Hardship Affidavit form at closing.

10. **Settlement of a Debt.** The proposed transaction represents our attempt to reach a settlement of the delinquent mortgage. There is no guarantee that the Contract will be approved or, if approved, the transaction will be successful. In the event the Contract is not approved, or, if approved, the transaction is unsuccessful, the Servicer may exercise all remedies under the mortgage, including foreclosure.

11. **Possible Income Tax Considerations.** We will report the difference between the remaining amount of principal you owe and the amount that we receive from the sale to the Internal Revenue Service (IRS) on Form 1099C, as debt forgiveness. In some cases, debt forgiveness could be taxed as income. The amount, if any, we pay you or your Tenant for moving expenses may also be reported as income. We suggest that you contact the IRS or your tax preparer to determine if you may have any tax liability.

12. **Credit Bureau Reporting.** We will follow standard industry practice and report to the major credit reporting agencies that your mortgage was settled for less than the full payment. We have no control over, or responsibility for, the impact of this report on your credit score. To learn more about the potential impact of a short sale on your credit, you may want to go to http://www.ftc.gov/bcp/edu/pubs/consumer/credit/cre24.shtm.

Important Program Information
MAKING HOME AFFORDABLE

If you have questions, please contact us directly between the hours of [insert hours] at [insert toll free number.]

_____   _____
Signature of Servicer Representative   Title

_____   _____
Printed Name of Servicer Representative   Date

If you would like to speak with a counselor about this program, call the Homeowner's HOPE™ Hotline 1-888-995-HOPE (4673). The Homeowner's HOPE™ Hotline offers free HUD-certified counseling services and is available 24/7 in English and Spanish. Other languages are available by appointment.

NOTICE TO BORROWER

Be advised that any documents and information you submit to your servicer in connection with the Making Home Affordable Program are under penalty of perjury. Any misstatement of material fact made in the completion of these documents including but not limited to misstatement regarding your occupancy in your home, hardship circumstances, and/or income, expenses, or assets will subject you to potential criminal investigation and prosecution for the following crimes: perjury, false statements, mail fraud, and wire fraud. The information contained in these documents is subject to examination and verification. Any potential misrepresentation will be referred to the appropriate law enforcement authority for investigation and prosecution. By returning documents or information described in this Notice you certify, represent and agree that:" Under penalty of perjury, all documents and information I have provided to Lender in connection with the Making Home Affordable Program, including the documents and information regarding my eligibility for the program, are true and correct."

If you are aware of fraud, waste, abuse, mismanagement or misrepresentations affiliated with the Troubled Asset Relief Program, please contact the SIGTARP Hotline by calling 1-877-SIG-2009 (toll-free), 202-622-4559 (fax), or www.sigtarp.gov. Mail can be sent Hotline Office of the Special Inspector General for Troubled Asset Relief Program, 1801 L St. NW, Washington, DC 20220.

APPENDIX

H

Non-owner Occupant (Tenant) Certification

Making Home Affordable Program
Non-Owner Occupant Certification

You are the occupant of a property that is being sold or transferred in conjunction with the U.S. Department of the Treasury's Home Affordable Foreclosure Alternative (HAFA) Program. Because you will be required to vacate the property as a condition of the sale or transfer, you may be eligible to receive $3,000 in relocation assistance. If you wish to be considered for this assistance, you must complete and sign this form and return it to the owner of the property (Owner).

OCCUPANT INFORMATION

OCCUPANT'S NAME	CO-OCCUPANT'S NAME

PROPERTY ADDRESS (include city, state and zip)

I certify that I currently occupy the property described above (the Property) as a principal residence and, to the best of my knowledge, I am required to vacate the Property as a condition of the pending sale or transfer.

DODD-FRANK CERTIFICATION

The following information is requested by the federal government in accordance with the Dodd-Frank Wall Street Reform and Consumer Protection Act (Pub. L. 111-203). **You are required to furnish this information.** The law provides that no person shall be eligible to begin receiving assistance from the Making Home Affordable Program (MHA), authorized under the Emergency Economic Stabilization Act of 2008 (12 U.S.C. 5201 et seq.), or any other mortgage assistance program authorized or funded by that Act, if such person, in connection with a mortgage or real estate transaction, has been convicted, within the last 10 years, of any one of the following: (A) felony larceny, theft, fraud, or forgery, (B) money laundering or (C) tax evasion.

I certify that I have not been convicted within the last 10 years of any one of the following in connection with a mortgage or real estate transaction:

      (a) felony larceny, theft, fraud, or forgery,
      (b) money laundering or
      (c) tax evasion.

I understand that the servicer of the mortgage loan secured by the Property (the Servicer), the U.S. Department of the Treasury (Treasury), or their respective agents may investigate the accuracy of my statements by performing routine background checks, including automated searches of federal, state and county databases, to confirm that I have not been convicted of such crimes. I also understand that knowingly submitting false information may violate Federal law. This certification is effective on the earlier of the date listed below or the date this form is received by the Servicer.

ACKNOWLEDGEMENT AND AGREEMENT

1. I authorize and give permission to the Servicer, Treasury, and their respective agents, to assemble and use a current consumer report to investigate my eligibility for HAFA relocation assistance, the accuracy of my statements and any documentation that I may provide in connection with requesting HAFA relocation assistance. I understand that these consumer reports may include, without limitation, a credit report, and be assembled and used at any point to assess my eligibility.

2. I understand that if I have engaged in fraud or if it is determined that any of my statements or any information contained in the documentation that I provide are materially false and that I was ineligible for relocation assistance under HAFA, the Servicer, Treasury, or their respective agents may seek remedies available at law and in equity, such as recouping any assistance I previously received.

3. I understand that the Servicer will collect and record personal information that I submit, including, but not limited to, my name, address, social security number and date of birth. I understand and consent to the Servicer's disclosure of my personal information and the terms of any assistance I may receive under MHA to Treasury and its agents, Fannie Mae and Freddie Mac in connection with their responsibilities under MHA, companies that perform support services in conjunction with MHA, any investor, insurer, guarantor, or servicer that owns, insures, guarantees, or services the mortgage loan(s) secured by the Property, and to any HUD-certified housing counselor assisting Owner.

4. I understand that the Owner may, but is not required to, request relocation assistance on my behalf. I authorize the Owner to submit this Certification to the Servicer in connection with any such request, along with any other documentation that the Servicer may require, and I authorize the Servicer to disclose to the Owner the results of any inquiry completed in conjunction with said Certifications and documentation.

The undersigned certifies under penalty of perjury that all statements in this document are true and correct.

▸ _____   _____   _____   _____
   Occupant Signature   Social Security Number   Date of Birth   Date

▸ _____   _____   _____   _____
   Co-Occupant Signature   Social Security Number   Date of Birth   Date

NOTICE TO OCCUPANTS

Be advised that by signing this document you understand that any documents and information you submit in connection with the Making Home Affordable Program are under penalty of perjury. Any misstatement of material fact made in the completion of these documents including but not limited to misstatement regarding your occupancy in the Property, will subject you to potential criminal investigation and prosecution for the following crimes: perjury, false statements, mail fraud, and wire fraud. The information contained in these documents is subject to examination and verification. Any potential misrepresentation will be referred to the appropriate law enforcement authority for investigation and prosecution. By signing this document you certify, represent and agree that: "Under penalty of perjury, all documents and information I have provided in connection with the Making Home Affordable Program, including the documents and information regarding my eligibility for relocation assistance under HAFA, are true and correct."

If you are aware of fraud, waste, abuse, mismanagement or misrepresentations affiliated with the Troubled Asset Relief Program, please contact the SIGTARP Hotline by calling 1-877-SIG-2009 (toll-free), 202-622-4559 (fax), or www.sigtarp.gov and provide them with your name, the Owner's name, the property address and reason for escalation. Mail can be sent to Hotline Office of the Special Inspector General for Troubled Asset Relief Program, 1801 L St. NW, Washington, DC 20220.

APPENDIX

I

Third party Authorization

HELPING YOU STAY IN YOUR HOME.

Third Party Authorization Form

_____   _____
Mortgage Lender/Servicer Name   **[Account][Loan] Number**

The undersigned Borrower and Co-Borrower (if any) (individually and collectively, "Borrower" or "I"), authorize the above mortgage lender/servicer and its successors and assigns (individually and collectively, "Servicer") and the following third parties

_____   _____
[Counseling Agency]   **[Agency Contact Name and Phone Number]**

_____   _____
[State HFA Entity]   **[State HFA Contact Name and Phone Number]**

_____   _____
[Other Third Party]   **[Third Party Contact Name and Phone Number]**

_____
[Relationship of Other Third Party to Borrower and Co-Borrower]

(individually and collectively, "Third Party") to obtain, share, release, discuss, and otherwise provide to and with each other public and non-public personal information contained in or related to the mortgage loan of the Borrower. This information may include (but is not limited to) the name, address, telephone number, social security number, credit score, credit report, income, government monitoring information, loss mitigation application status, account balances, program eligibility, and payment activity of the Borrower. I also understand and consent to the disclosure of my personal information and the terms of any agreements under the Making Home Affordable or Hardest Hit Fund Programs by Servicer or State HFA to the U.S. Department of the Treasury or their agents in connection with their responsibilities under the Emergency Economic Stabilization Act.

The Servicer will take reasonable steps to verify the identity of a Third Party, but has no responsibility or liability to verify the identity of such Third Party. The Servicer also has no responsibility or liability for what a Third Party does with such information.

Before signing this Third Party Authorization, beware of foreclosure rescue scams!

- It is expected that a HUD-approved housing counselor, HFA representative or other authorized third party will work directly with your lender/mortgage servicer.
- Please visit http://makinghomeaffordable.gov/counselor.html to verify you are working with a HUD-approved housing counseling agency.
- Beware of anyone who asks you to pay a fee in exchange for a counseling service or modification of a delinquent loan.

This Third-Party Authorization is valid when signed by all borrowers and co-borrowers named on the mortgage and until the Servicer receives a written revocation signed by any borrower or co-borrower.

I UNDERSTAND AND AGREE WITH THE TERMS OF THIS THIRD-PARTY AUTHORIZATION:

Borrower   **Co-Borrower**

_____   _____
Printed Name   **Printed Name**

_____   _____
Signature   **Signature**

_____   _____

HELPING YOU STAY IN YOUR HOME.

THIRD PARTY AUTHORIZATION FORM COMPLETION GUIDELINES

[Mortgage Lender/Servicer Name] ("Servicer") - The name of the banking institution servicing the account.

[Account] [Loan] Number - The account or loan number assigned to the mortgage. You can find this on the mortgage statement.

[Counseling Agency] - The name of the Counseling Agency assisting the Borrower(s).

[Agency Contact Name and Phone Number] - The name and telephone number of the primary point of contact at the Counseling Agency.

[State HFA Entity] – The name of the State Housing Finance Agency (if applicable).

[State HFA Contact Name and Phone Number] - The name and telephone number of the primary point of contact at the State Housing Finance Agency (if applicable).

[Other Third Party] – The name of the Real Estate Agency, Attorney/Law Offices, Trusted Advisors, non-borrower spouse or other person/entity (if applicable).

[Third Party Contact Name and Phone Number] - The name and telephone number of the primary point of contact of the Other Third Party.

[Relationship of Other Third Party to Borrower and Co-Borrower] - If applicable or needed, provide additional information on the relationship of the Other Third Party to the Borrower(s).

[Borrower]

> **Printed Name** – The first and last name of the Borrower named on the mortgage. [Parties on the Deed but not on the Mortgage should not sign the LOA].
>
> **Signature** –Borrower's signature.
>
> **Date** – The date of the signature.

[Co-Borrower]

> **Printed Name** – The first and last name of any Co-Borrower named on the mortgage. [Parties on the Deed but not on the Mortgage should not sign the LOA].
>
> **Signature** – Co-Borrower's signature.
>
> **Date** - The date of the signature.

APPENDIX

J

Escalation by Third Party

Help for America's Homeowners

Case Submission

Please e-mail this document to **escalations@hmpadmin.com**

Date: [   ] *(mm/dd/yyyy)*

HOMEOWNER INFORMATION

Homeowner Name: [   ]

Property Address: [   ]

Phone: [   ]

Email Address: [   ]

Last 4 digits of SS#: [   ]

MHA Program: [choose one   ]

Property Owner Mailing Address:
[   ]

SERVICER INFORMATION

Servicer Name: [   ]

Servicer Loan #: [   ]
(required to escalate)

Investor Type:
[choose one   ]

ESCALATION INFORMATION

Name: [   ]

Contact Name: [   ]

Contact Phone #: [   ]

Contact Email: [   ]

Relationship to Homeowner: [   ]

Are you charging a fee?

Yes   No

If so, how much? [   ]

Property Type:

Owner Occupied   Second/Seasonal Home

Rented   Vacant

Case Type: *(choose one)*

Servicer did not assess the borrower for the applicable MHA Program according to Program Guidelines

Initiation or continuance of foreclosure actions in violation of Program Guidelines, and there is no foreclosure sale scheduled to occur in the next 14 days

Initiation or continuance of foreclosure actions in violation of Program Guidelines, and foreclosure is imminent (i.e., sale scheduled to occur in the next 14 days)

Inappropriate program denial

Other

If other, please describe:

[   ]

Foreclosure Date *(if applicable):* [   ]

Eviction Date *(if applicable):* [   ]

Description of Concerns:

[   ]

** If you/the homeowner was denied assistance under the Making Home Affordable Program, please provide a copy of the Non-Approval Notice the homeowner received.

Third Party Authorization Form

Please provide a copy of the authorization form executed by the homeowner that authorizes us to communicate with you about the homeowner's mortgage loan and authorizes you to act on their behalf with respect to assistance on their mortgage loan. The MHA Third Party Authorization Form is available as the 2nd page of this Case Submission form or at http://www.hmpadmin.com under "Programs" - "Home Affordable Modification Program" - "Borrower Documents" - "General Solicitation Offers".
You can send a copy of the Non-Approval Notice and the authorization form as an email attachment or by fax to 1-240-699-3883.
Note: The information requested needs to be sent from your organization's email account, not a public ISP (such as AOL, Yahoo, gmail, etc.). For future communication, please retain the servicer loan number for reference to this case.

APPENDIX

K

Making Home Affordable Programs

- Home Affordable Foreclosure Alternatives Program (HAFA)
  http://www.makinghomeaffordable.gov/programs/exit-gracefully/Pages/hafa.aspx
- Home Affordable Modification Program (HAMP)
  http://www.makinghomeaffordable.gov/programs/lower-payments/Pages/hamp.aspx
- Principal Reduction Alternative (PRA)
  http://www.makinghomeaffordable.gov/programs/lower-payments/Pages/pra.aspx
- Second Lien Modification Program (2MP)
  http://www.makinghomeaffordable.gov/programs/second-mortgage-help/Pages/default.aspx
- Home Affordable Unemployment Program (UP)
  http://www.makinghomeaffordable.gov/programs/unemployed-help/Pages/up.aspx
- Home Affordable Refinance Program (HARP)
  http://www.makinghomeaffordable.gov/programs/lower-rates/Pages/harp.aspx
- Fannie Mae Home Affordable Modification Program (HAMP)
  http://knowyouroptions.com/modify/home-affordable-modification-program
- Freddie Mac Home Affordable Modification Program (HAMP)
  http://www.freddiemac.com/mortgage_help/home_affordable_modification.html
- Housing Finance Agency Fund for the Hardest Hit Housing Markets (HHF)
  http://www.makinghomeaffordable.gov/programs/unemployed-help/Pages/hhf.aspx

- FHA Home Affordable Modification Program (FHA-HAMP)
  http://www.makinghomeaffordable.gov/programs/lower-payments/Pages/fha-hamp.aspx
- Second Lien Modification Program for FHA Loans (FHA-2LP)
  http://www.makinghomeaffordable.gov/programs/lower-rates/Pages/fha2lp.aspx
- FHA Refinance for Borrowers with Negative Equity (FHA Short Refinance)
  http://www.makinghomeaffordable.gov/programs/lower-rates/Pages/short-refinance.aspx
- USDA's Special Loan Servicing
  http://www.makinghomeaffordable.gov/programs/lower-payments/Pages/rd-hamp.aspx
- Veteran's Affairs Home Affordable Modification (VA-HAMP)
  http://www.makinghomeaffordable.gov/programs/lower-payments/Pages/va-hamp.aspx

APPENDIX

L

Scam Avoidance

Making Home Affordable Statement[iii]

Beware of Foreclosure Rescue Scams!

Real Help is Free!

Foreclosure rescue and mortgage modification scams are a growing problem that could cost you thousands of dollars—or even your home.

Scammers make promises that they can't keep, such as guaranteeing to "save" your home or lower your mortgage, usually for a fee, often pretending that they have direct contact with your mortgage servicer—which they do not.

But the federal government provides the help you need for free!

Just call 888-995-HOPE (4673) for information about The Making Home Affordable Program ® and to speak with a HUD-approved housing counselor. Assistance is available free, 24-7, in 160 languages.

Tips to Avoid Scams:

1. Beware of anyone who asks you to pay a fee in exchange for counseling services or the modification of a delinquent loan.

[iii]http://www.makinghomeaffordable.gov/learning-center/Pages/beware.aspx.

2. Beware of people who pressure you to sign papers immediately or who try to convince you that they can "save" your home if you sign or transfer over the deed to your house.

3. Do not sign over the deed to your property to any organization or individual unless you are working directly with your mortgage company to forgive your debt.

4. Never make a mortgage payment to anyone other than your mortgage company without their approval.

What to Do if You Have Been the Victim of a Scam

If you believe you have been the victim of a scam, you should file a complaint with the Federal Trade Commission (FTC). Visit the FTC's online Complaint Assistant or call 877-FTC-HELP (877-382-4357) for assistance in English or Spanish.

StopFraud.gov Statement[iv]

To Report Mortgage Fraud or Loan Scams:

Federal Bureau of Investigation

Phone: 1-800-CALLFBI (225-5324)

Online Tips: FBI Tips and Public Leads Form

To file a complaint with the FBI contact the nearest FBI field office. Locations are listed at www.fbi.gov/contactus.htm or https://tips.fbi.gov/ or for major cases, you can also report information by calling toll-free number 1-800-CALLFBI (225-5324).

Housing and Urban Development (HUD) Office of the Inspector General Hotline

Phone: (800) 347-3735

Fax: (202) 708-4829

Email: hotline@hudoig.gov

Address: HUD OIG Hotline (GFI), 451 7th Street, SW, Washington, DC 20410

PreventLoanScams.org: A project of the Lawyers' Committee for Civil Rights Under the Law

Website: PreventLoanScams.org

Phone: 1-888-995-HOPE

PreventLoanScams.org - was launched to serve as a nationwide clearinghouse for loan modification scam information on complaints filed, laws and regulations,

---

[iv]http://www.stopfraud.gov/report.html#mortgage.

and enforcement actions. If you think you've been scammed or approached by a company or individual promising to help you with your foreclosure, report it today.

Federal Trade Commission (FTC): Complaint Assistant

Web Site (Spanish): https://www.ftccomplaintassistant.gov/Consumer_HomeES.htm

Phone (for complaints against companies, organizations, or business practices): (877) FTC-**HELP**

Phone (for complaints about identity theft): (877) ID-THEFT

Email Address (for complaints about spam or phishing): spam@uce.gov

The Federal Trade Commission collects complaints about fraud, companies, business practices, identity theft, and episodes of violence in the media.

APPENDIX

M

Glossary of Terms

The following descriptions and explanations are offered by the author for quick reference in the context of this book. They have no legal significance. Before relying on any definition, ensure that it is correct in the context and jurisdiction where it is being used.

Acceleration. Regardless of its actual due date, a loan in default may be called due, which is the first step in a foreclosure. Correcting the default, which can be accomplished by loan modification, ends the threat of foreclosure.

Acknowledgment of Request for Short Sale (ARSS). A lender's confirmation of receipt from a borrower of a sales contract that results in a short sale, which initiates the analysis and results in approval, disapproval, or a counteroffer.

Adjustable Rate Mortgage. Some loans are designed with an interest rate that changes from time to time. The periodic changes are determined by adding a fixed margin to a variable index rate, which reflects market conditions and allows lenders to maintain a current yield. Changes may be limited by lifetime and period caps, which may be maximums or minimums. All elements—index, margin, caps, and period—are defined in the promissory note.

Affidavit. A written statement affirming that a document is true and accurate.

Agreement Not to Foreclose. Temporarily suspends or delays foreclosure proceedings when a condition of default exists. Typically, it is an unwritten temporary suspension during a pending modification. A formal proposal would be strengthened by evidence of disclosure or loan closing document irregularities, or predatory lending practices.

Amortization. When loan payments include both interest and principal, each payment reduces the outstanding loan balance. As the loan balance declines, less of the payment goes to interest and more goes to principal, thus accelerating the reduction of the loan balance over time. If paid completely, the loan is fully amortizing.

Balloon Payment. When a loan is not fully amortizing, a principal balance remains at the end of the loan term, and it is due in a lump-sum payment. See *Amortization*.

Bankruptcy. Forgiveness of debt through a judicial process. When bankruptcy is a consideration, its procedures and consequences should always be discussed with qualified legal counsel and financial advisors.

Capitalized Principal Balance. Includes the unpaid principal balance (UPB) of a loan plus payments advanced by the lender for such expenses as property tax or insurance not paid by a borrower. It might also include the interest portion of missed payments, but it must exclude late fees or administrative costs if a modification occurs.

Cash Reserves. Also known as liquid assets, cash reserves are money that can be withdrawn within a short period of time. Obvious ones are checking and savings accounts. Others are sellable stocks, bonds, mutual funds, money market funds, and, for HAMP purposes, certificates of deposit of any maturity. Excluded are retirement accounts, whether self-administered (IRA, 401(k), Keogh, etc.) or other-administered (employer, pension), and deferred compensation or stock options. See also *Emergency Reserve*.

CheckMyNPV.com. Web-based self-service tool for borrowers and their advisors to independently predict potential net present value eligibility for the Home Affordable Modification Program (HAMP). Go to https://checkmynpv.com/.

Claim Advance. If the mortgage is insured, the insurer may consider an interest-free loan to bring the account current, avoiding a lender's claim for a loss from foreclosure or short sale. Full repayment of the interim loan might be delayed for several years.

Combined Loan-to-Value Ratio (CLTV). Calculated by dividing the total combined senior and junior loan amounts by the property value. See *Loan-to-Value Ratio*.

Current Monthly Mortgage Payment. The mortgage payment including property tax and insurance prior to modification. See *Mortgage Payment*.

Current Monthly P&I. Shorthand for "principal and interest." See *Monthly P&I*.

Debt. As used to calculate the debt coverage ratio, it is the current principal and interest portion of the current monthly mortgage payment for the loan to be modified.

Debt Coverage Ratio. The relationship of net income to loan payments, indicating the income "cushion" that remains after making those payments. Used in Fannie Mae and other imminent default screens.

Debt-to-Income Ratio. See *Gross Expense-to-Income Ratio*.

Deed-in-Lieu of Foreclosure. Often simply called "deed-in-lieu." Borrower voluntarily surrenders ownership of the property to lender, and the debt is forgiven. This option may be unavailable if other liens encumber title to the property (for example, judgments of other creditors, junior mortgages, IRS, or state tax liens). Sometimes referred to colloquially as "turning over the keys."

Deed of Trust. Also known as a trust deed, a form of mortgage that allows for enforcement of the lender's claim according to a predefined and streamlined procedure sanctioned by state law. In a foreclosure, the trust deed allows a lender (through a trustee) to sell the underlying property without judicial action, but it then precludes recourse to borrower's other assets. See *Single Action Rule*.

Deficiency Judgment. When a loan is not paid in full, a deficiency results. If the lender sues the borrower for the deficit amount and wins, then the court enters a deficiency judgment, which may be enforced as any other award of the court. See *Single Action Rule*.

Disposable Net Income. Income left after payroll deductions and all credit obligations are satisfied, including housing and living expenses, but excluding the mortgage payment to be modified.

Eligibility. The borrower, the mortgage, the property, and the lender must meet a set of criteria before a loan may be considered for modification under HAMP.

Emergency Reserve. Equal to three times monthly "debt payments," according to HAMP. Fannie Mae limits the reserve to three times monthly "housing expenses," which is a lower cash reserve amount. See also *Cash Reserves*.

Equity. The difference between the value of property and the encumbrances, liens, loans, and other claims against the property. This net value is the ownership interest in the property. If it is a negative amount, the terms "negative equity" and "underwater" are commonly used.

Escalation. The process used by a borrower or advisor to challenge and correct a lender's negative decision.

Escrow. A disinterested third party is appointed to hold items of value deposited by one party with instructions to deliver those items to another party on the occurrence of a predetermined event. An example is the sale and purchase of a home. The seller deposits a conveyance deed and the buyer deposits (or arranges for a lender to deposit) funds equaling the purchase price. Each instructs escrow to deliver the deposited items to the other when all the conditions of the sale and purchase are complete.

Escrow Account. An accumulating amount paid by a borrower monthly and held by the lender to pay annual or semiannual property tax and insurance premium payments. Sometimes referred to as an impound account.

Estimated Principal Balance. The loan amount used to determine the modified payments. Includes the balance at time of modification, plus past due interest and escrow amounts paid by the lender on behalf of the borrower. It may not include late fees and other administrative costs. See *Capitalized Principal Balance.*

Fannie Mae. Founded in 1938, the Federal National Mortgage Association, or Fannie Mae, is one of two government-sponsored enterprises used to underwrite trillions of dollars of mortgages, allowing the private financial markets to fund the American dream of homeownership. After suffering substantial losses due to deteriorated real estate and mortgage markets, Fannie Mae was placed into conservatorship in September 2008 under the Federal Housing Finance Agency. See also *Freddie Mac.*

Federal Housing Finance Agency. Conservator for Fannie Mae and Freddie Mac.

Forbearance. A reduction or suspension of payments with the lender's agreement, while another form of relief is being negotiated or until a temporary difficulty ends.

Forbearance of Interest. A waiver of interest on a portion of the loan principal to reduce monthly payments to an affordable and sustainable level. That portion of principal must be repaid, but without interest.

Foreclosure. A statutory procedure that begins with a borrower's default in payments on a loan and ends with the sale of the property securing the loan. The sale proceeds go first to paying the costs of sale, then to paying the loan. If the proceeds are insufficient to satisfy the loan, state law determines whether the borrower may be held personally liable. See *Judicial Foreclosure*, *Single Action Rule*, and *Trustee Sale.*

Foreclosure Alternatives. Includes modification, principal forgiveness and forbearance, short sale and deed-in-lieu of foreclosure within the Making Home Affordable program. Refer to Appendix K, "Making Home Affordable Programs," page 97. Usually also available as proprietary programs at individual servicers.

Forgiveness. A permanent reduction of the unpaid principal balance (UPB) of a loan. See *Principal Forgiveness.*

Freddie Mac. Founded in 1970, the Federal Home Loan Mortgage Corporation, or Freddie Mac, is one of two government-sponsored enterprises used to underwrite trillions of dollars of mortgages, allowing the private financial markets to bankroll the American dream of homeowners. In September 2008, after suffering substantial losses due to deteriorated real estate and mortgage markets, Freddie Mac was placed into conservatorship under the Federal Housing Finance Agency. See also *Fannie Mae.*

Government-Sponsored Enterprises (GSE). See *Fannie Mae* and *Freddie Mac.*

Gross Expense-to-Income Ratio. Compares income from all sources with all credit and most living expenses, and measures relative debt burden, overall ability to meet obligations, viability of the loan modification beyond its impact on monthly mortgage payments, and responsible use of borrowed money. Also referred to as the "monthly debt ratio," "debt-to-income ratio," and "'back-end' ratio."

Gross Income. All income from any source, before withholding or deductions, including earnings received from self-employment and nonemployment sources such as a pension or public assistance. A component of the monthly mortgage payment ratio.

Hardship Affidavit. A standardized form for describing the "events" that contribute to a borrower's difficulty in making mortgage payments. A central component of eligibility, a borrower must submit the hardship events in writing.

Homeowner Association (HOA). The governing board for a condominium planned unit development (PUD), or other group of homeowners gathered for a common purpose. Fees are collected from homeowners for administering the group and improving, maintaining, and repairing the property. Unpaid fees may become a lien against the individual owner's property.

Housing Expense. Occasionally used interchangeably with monthly mortgage payment. See *Mortgage Payment*.

Imminent Risk of Default. The likelihood that a borrower who is current on payments will be unable to continue making timely payments. Either the lender must find a borrower to be "at risk" or a borrower must be 60 or more days late (seriously delinquent) for the borrower to be eligible for modification. Also referred to as reasonably foreseeable default.

Impound Account. See *Escrow Account*.

Income. See *Gross Income*.

Initial Package. Begins the HAMP evaluation process. It consists of the Request for Mortgage Assistance (RMA) form, IRS Form 4506-T or 4506T-EZ, and evidence of income.

Interest Rate Cap. The Freddie Mac 30-year fixed rate at the time of the modification determines the maximum rate for the modified loan.

Investor. In this book, "investor" refers to the actual owner of a mortgage, which has the right to receive repayment of the loan amount and interest on the outstanding principal. In the past, the financial institution lending the money was also the investor, on behalf of its depositors. Recently, money has been raised in financial markets through mortgage-backed securities (securities backed by a pool of similar mortgages), and the issuer of the securities is now the investor. See *Loan Servicer*.

Judicial Foreclosure. An action in court to enforce a lender's secured interest in real estate. In effect, it is a lawsuit for breach of contract when a borrower defaults on the promissory note. A costly and time-consuming alternative, it is seldom used when the mortgage includes a separate enforcement provision, as in a deed of trust.

Lender. In this book, "lender" refers generically to the originator, servicer, and/or investor of the mortgage. Specifically, it refers to the recipient of a borrower's monthly payments and request for modification.

Lien. A claim against property, typically to ensure repayment of a debt, but also to ensure payment for certain services to improve the property (for example, a mechanic's lien for construction, repairs, and materials) or to ensure payment of charges against the property (for example, a tax lien for unpaid property taxes).

Loan Servicer. See *Servicer*. See also *Lender*; those terms are used interchangeably with loan servicer in this book.

Loan-to-Value (LTV) Ratio. Calculated by dividing the senior loan amount by the property value. The lower the result, the less risk there is to a lender and the more equity there is vested in the owner. Any result greater than 100 percent, however, is commonly referred to as negative equity or being underwater.

Modification Agreement. The agreement between a lender and a borrower that permanently changes the promissory note. It becomes effective upon completion of the trial period.

Modification Evaluator. A tool to help borrowers determine whether they might be eligible for a HAMP. Go to http://makinghomeaffordable.gov/evaluator.html.

Monthly Debt Ratio. See *Gross Expense-to-Income Ratio*.

Monthly Disposable Net Income. Income left after the satisfaction of payroll deductions and all credit obligations, including housing and living expenses, but excluding the mortgage payment to be modified. See *Disposable Net Income*.

Monthly Gross Expenses. Though HAMP identifies specific expense items, it generally includes mortgage payments, other housing expenses, and credit obligations.

Monthly Gross Income. See *Gross Income*.

Monthly Mortgage Payment. See *Mortgage Payment*.

Monthly Mortgage Payment Ratio. See *Mortgage Payment Ratio*.

Monthly Obligations. Include personal debts, revolving (credit card) accounts, installment loans, and household or living expenses.

Monthly P&I. The principal and interest payment that traditionally has been considered the mortgage payment. However, for HAMP purposes, P&I is a component of the monthly mortgage payment, which also include escrow account payments. See *Amortization*. Contrast with *Negative Amortization* and interest-only payments.

Mortgage. A lien or claim against real property (real estate) to ensure repayment of a loan, almost always for the purpose of buying the property, refinancing a previous loan, or liquidating equity accumulated from a down payment or value appreciation. The borrower owns the real estate, but the lender has a claim or interest in the real estate, specifically the right to sell it and collect what is owed from the sale proceeds if the borrower does not repay the loan as agreed. The term "mortgage" usually refers to both the loan agreement (promissory note) and the security instrument (mortgage or deed of trust).

Mortgage Payment. Combines the principal and interest paid to the lender, plus monthly allotments for property taxes and insurance, homeowner association fees, and certain other assessments. It does not include payments for any second mortgage or for mortgage insurance, which are included in debt and in monthly obligations. Also see *Target Monthly Mortgage Payment*.

Mortgage Payment Ratio. Calculates the portion of income needed to pay housing expenses by dividing the monthly mortgage payment by gross monthly income. It is commonly referred to as the housing-to-income or front-end ratio. See *Target Monthly Mortgage Payment Ratio*.

Negative Amortization. When loan payments are less than interest owed, and the unpaid interest is added to the loan balance, the balance increases. This is the opposite of amortization, which reduces the loan balance.

Negative Equity. See *Equity*. A property with negative equity is said to be underwater.

Net Income. See *Disposable Net Income*.

Net Present Value (NPV). The current value of future costs and benefits (cash flow) to a lender from modifying a mortgage versus foreclosing on it.

Net Present Value (NPV) Input Values. Individual credit, property, loan, and similar unique variables used when evaluating a borrower in the NPV Test.

Net Present Value (NPV) Test. The process of determining the net present value of a loan, and comparing the results. If modification is more beneficial to the lender than foreclosure, then the results are "positive" and the lender is required by HAMP to modify. Otherwise, the lender may or may not modify, but it should consider foreclosure alternatives.

Nonapproval. Denial by a lender of a request for modification due to a borrower's ineligibility or negative NPV Test findings, sometimes for failure to arrive at a viable monthly mortgage payment using the standard modification waterfall.

Nonapproval Notice. Written explanation to the borrower from the lender that lists the reasons for denying a request for modification.

Nonrecourse Agreement. Lender agrees not to make claims against assets of a borrower other than the property to compensate for any deficiency. Might be imposed by statute.

Payment Constant. A number that corresponds to an interest rate and amortization term. The fully amortizing payment for any loan amount, at that rate and term, can be found by multiplying the loan amount by the payment constant.

Payment Reduction Estimator. A tool available to help an eligible borrower estimate the payment resulting from a modification. Go to http://makinghomeaffordable. gov/payment_reduction_estimator.html.

Pooling and Servicing Agreement. Governs the relationship between a loan servicer and investor. It may restrict loan servicers in applying HAMP to modify loans, even if the servicer has entered a Servicer Participant Agreement.

Pre-Foreclosure Sale. See *Short Sale*.

Principal Balance. The amount of a loan that remains unpaid. Same as unpaid principal balance (UPB).

Principal Forbearance. A portion of the loan on which monthly payments are not required and interest is not charged (non-interest bearing). It is intended to further reduce the modified monthly mortgage payment. The amount must be paid as a balloon payment when the loan is due. Contrast with *Principal Forgiveness*.

Principal Forgiveness. An actual reduction of the outstanding loan amount. Because the principal is forgiven, it will not be due in the future, and this also effectively reduces the monthly payment.

Promissory Note. The agreement or contract that defines the terms and conditions of a loan and its repayment. A promissory note for a real estate loan should always be secured by a mortgage or deed of trust, which serves to enforce the promise to repay.

Proposed Principal Balance. A tactic suggested in this book to reduce the estimated (capitalized) principal balance on which modified payments are calculated. It would require principal forgiveness by the lender.

Qualification. In this book, qualification refers to the credit analysis or underwriting of a borrower's ability to make modified loan payments. Contrast with *Eligibility*, which involves a set of threshold criteria.

Reasonably Foreseeable Default. See *Imminent Risk of Default*.

Redefault. After modifying a delinquent loan, the borrower misses the modified payments and again becomes delinquent.

Reinstatement. Payment by a specific date of all back interest and principal owed, in exchange for "reinstating" the loan to its pre-default status. Reinstatement will take the loan out of delinquency status, but it will not reverse previous delinquency reports to credit bureaus. It is typically combined with forbearance and the expectation of a windfall (e.g., a bonus, investment, insurance settlement, or tax refund).

Repayment Plan. An agreement between the lender and borrower that apportions delinquent amounts to subsequent payments until all back interest, late fees, and other included amounts are paid. Results in a temporary or permanent increase in payments. May also be used to repay a forbearance amount. See *Forbearance*.

Request for Modification and Affidavit (RMA). Former name of Request for Mortgage Assistance.

Request for Mortgage Assistance (RMA). Principal form in the Initial Package to commence consideration for Making Home Affordable mortgage relief.

Requestor. The borrower or authorized third party who escalates a disputed case.

Servicer. Collects payments as the investor's agent, keeping its fees, and then passing through the remainder. In this book, the servicer is also referred to as the "lender."

Servicer Participant Agreement (SPA). The agreement entered into by loan servicers and lenders that participate in HAMP. In return for complying with HAMP guidelines, they are entitled to receive incentive payments from the federal government.

Short Payoff. The lender agrees to accept less than the full amount owed and the difference (shortfall) is forgiven, usually resulting in a lower loss to the lender than foreclosure would.

Short Refinance. Refinancing to a more affordable mortgage by a qualified borrower that results in a short payoff, often due to a decline in property value. It has the effect of a principal reduction and is unusual. Complicated by any junior lien or judgment.

Short Sale. A conventional sale when the net proceeds are less than the loan balance, resulting in a short payoff. The lender agrees to accept less than the full amount owed, releases the lien (security interest) so title may pass unencumbered to the buyer, and might waive (forgive) the unpaid portion of the loan principal (deficiency or shortfall).

Short Sale Notice. The lender's agreement relating to a borrower's request for a short sale, which sets an acceptable price (minimum net sale proceeds) and promises at least 120 days to market the property, during which a foreclosure sale may not occur.

Single Action Rule. In some states, a lender must choose either to foreclose based on the security instrument (mortgage or deed of trust) or to sue for breach of contract (promissory note), but it cannot do both. In almost every instance, residential lenders will foreclose, thereby eliminating a lawsuit and a deficiency judgment.

Single-Family Property. Any residential real estate with one to four units. In MHA language, it is not limited to a single-dwelling structure.

Standard Modification Waterfall. The sequence of steps required by HAMP to reduce the interest rate, extend the amortization term, and forbear principal as needed to arrive at a mortgage payment that is affordable and sustainable for the homeowner.

Target Monthly Mortgage Payment. The modified payment calculated by multiplying gross monthly income by the target monthly mortgage payment ratio, which may not be less than 31 percent. The payment totals the reduced principal and interest payment, plus the other listed expenses.

Target Monthly Mortgage Payment Ratio. The objective is to reduce the payment until this ratio closely approaches but does not fall below 31 percent. To determine the target monthly mortgage payment, multiply gross monthly income by the 31 percent and round up when applying the modified interest rate, amortization, and principal forbearance.

Trial Period. Precedes the actual loan modification. Typically lasts three months and involves a trial period plan and preparation of the final modification agreement.

Trial Period Plan. Defines the terms of a trial period, primarily modified payments and due dates. Modification requires completion of the trial period according to the plan.

Trust Deed. See *Deed of Trust*.

Trustee Sale. The foreclosure sale under a deed of trust. Also known as a non-judicial foreclosure, because it requires no further legal or judicial action for its enforcement.

Underwriting. The process of analyzing the ability to repay and the creditworthiness of an applicant for a loan or other extension or modification of credit.

Unpaid Principal Balance (UPB). The unpaid portion of a loan. Same as principal balance.

Index

About the Author

Dean Allen Kackley is a licensed attorney and real estate broker with a thorough knowledge of the federal Home Affordable Modification Program (HAMP). He counsels borrowers regarding mortgage relief options and represents them in loan workouts with their lenders. In addition to a wide variety of real estate transactions, his lending experience spans more than two decades.

After joining Wells Fargo Bank in 1985, then a "portfolio" lender that owned all its originated loans, Kackley helped to develop its residential mortgage business with his broad knowledge of underwriting, settlement, and servicing functions. He worked briefly for the Independent National Mortgage Corporation (IndyMac), a market-maker for mortgage-backed securities, mortgage pooling and servicing investments, and alternate and subprime loans.

In more than $250 million of sale, lease, and financing transactions, his experience involves residential, commercial, and land development properties, and hundreds of closings. A graduate of Yale University and the University of Kansas School of Law, Kackley writes with a passion, intelligence, understanding, and clarity that are rare for this kind of book. His practice is located in Napa Valley, California.